AN ANATOMY OF INSPIRATION

AN ANATOMY
OF INSPIRATION

by

ROSAMOND E. M. HARDING

(Ph.D., Litt.D., Cantab.)

With an Appendix on
THE BIRTH OF A POEM
BY
ROBERT B. M. NICHOLS

A New Impression of the
SECOND EDITION
with corrections

Routledge
Taylor & Francis Group

LONDON AND NEW YORK

Published by
FRANK CASS AND COMPANY LIMITED
2 Park Square, Milton Park, Abingdon, Oxon, OX14 4RN
by arrangement with W. Heffer and Sons Ltd.
711 Third Avenue, New York, NY 10017

Routledge is an imprint of the Taylor & Francis Group, an informa business

First issued in paperback 2016

First edition	1940
Second edition	1942
Third edition	1948
Reprint of Second edition (with minor corrections)	1967

Transferred to Digital Printing 2006

ISBN: 978-0-714-62060-2 (hbk)
ISBN: 978-1-138-99043-2 (pbk)

FRANCES MARY THORNHILL ASHTON:
with deep affection and gratitude

Preface to the First Edition

A number of books have been written dealing with the methods of work of authors and men of science ; and many scientific investigations are being made into the psychology of the creative mind. But, so far as we are aware, no serious attempt has yet been made to *classify* the enormous amount of historical data that exists relating to the 'mind in creation' which is to be found in letters, autobiographies, and eye-witness accounts. The result appears to be that scientists proceed with highly specialised investigations based often upon half-knowledge of historical facts and are baffled in consequence. We venture to suggest, therefore, that the first step to the investigation of the creative mind is the historical approach. That is not only the collection of historical data, which some laboratories have already attempted, but a careful classification of such material and the collection of everything available from the past as well as the present. If this was done there would then be a solid basis from which to start specialised scientific inquiry. Such historical research should be regarded as scientific and of psychological value and not merely read to pass away amusingly an idle half-hour.

The present small work is an attempt on a very modest scale at such a classification and must be looked upon as but a sketch for the picture which the author hopes may one day be completed. The sources from which the material has been drawn are letters, autobiographies, eye-witness accounts, contemporary biographies and the standard biographies, etc. Actual quotations are given when possible as more scientific and accurate. Religious inspiration, though there is an occasional reference to it, and occultism are outside the scope of this study.

The first chapter deals with the preparation for creative thought. In all great undertakings there is always the period of preparation ; the success of the adventure depends much on the care bestowed on preliminaries. The first chapter attempts to show, amongst other matters, the

standard of knowledge attained by those who have produced
work of lasting value.

There is, happily, much data to be gathered from letters
concerning the various stages of inspiration. The second
chapter is an attempt to codify this material. The suddenness with which a decisive idea presents itself to the mind ;
the crisis when 'ideas are shooting together,' the gradual
decline of inspiration when the mind becomes 'as a fading
coal' and composition actually begins, are dealt with in
detail. Nor have I neglected to mention such typical
experiences as the sense of possession when, as George Sand
declared, 'the other' took charge and Sidney Dobell felt
himself to be nothing more than a 'receiver' or 'mouth-
piece.' Of the remaining chapters : Chapter III deals with
those principles of procedure which are common to all
branches of the creative process. It is important to realise
that there is a definite technique ; a clearly marked 'path'
which is common to all types of creative thought. Chapters
IV and V deal with the special procedure for novel-writing,
poetry, music, painting and scientific research. In the final
chapter I have attempted to interpret the phenomena
according to my own theories.

I beg to tender my sincere thanks to Professor Bartlett,
Sc.D., F.R.S., for his great kindness in reading through this
book in typescript. His comments and advice have been
of the greatest value to me.

Finally, I desire to express my great indebtedness to the
courtesy of those Publishing Houses, the names of whom
are given below, for their very kind permission to quote
extracts from the books of which they are the publishers
(or owners of the copyright or successors to the firms by
whom the book was first published, etc.) as listed in the
Bibliography, pp. 150–172. Namely to Messrs. George Allen
& Unwin, Ltd.; Messrs. George Bell & Sons ; Messrs. Ernest
Benn, Ltd. ; Messrs. A. & C. Black, Ltd. ; Messrs. William
Blackwood & Sons, Ltd. (Edinburgh and London) ; Messrs.
Thornton Butterworth, Ltd. ; The Cambridge University
Press (Cambridge and London) ; Messrs. Jonathan Cape,
Ltd. ; Messrs. Chapman & Hall, Ltd. ; Messrs. Chatto &
Windus, and The Macmillan Company (New York) ; Messrs.

Constable & Co., Ltd.; Messrs. J. M. Dent & Sons, Ltd., and Messrs. E. P. Dutton & Co., Inc.; Messrs. Douglas & Foulis (Edinburgh); Messrs. Gerald Duckworth & Co., Ltd.; Messrs. Faber & Faber, Ltd.; *M.* Eugène Fasquelle, Bibliothèque Charpentier (Paris); *M.* Ernest Flammarion, Librairie Ernest Flammarion, Paris; Messrs. Funk & Wagnalls Company (New York and London); Messrs. Victor Gollancz, Ltd.; Messrs. Harper & Brothers (New York and London); Messrs. William Heinemann, Ltd.; Messrs. Hurst & Blackett, Ltd.; Messrs. Herbert Jenkins; Messrs. John Lane, The Bodley Head, Ltd.; Messrs. Little, Brown & Company (Boston, Mass.); Messrs. Longmans, Green & Co., Ltd.; The Richards Press, Ltd.; Messrs. Sampson Low, Marston & Co., Ltd.; Messrs. Sands & Co.; Messrs. Macmillan & Co., Ltd.; The Oxford University Press (London); The Clarendon Press (Oxford); Messrs. Putnam & Co., Ltd. (London and New York); Messrs. Martin Secker & Warburg, Ltd.; Messrs. A. Knopf (New York); Messrs. Novello & Co., Ltd.; Messrs. Thomas Nelson & Sons, Ltd.; The Swedenborg Society (London); Messrs. Taylor & Francis, Ltd.; The Rationalist Press Association, Ltd.; Messrs. George Routledge & Sons, Ltd.; The Yale University Press (New Haven, Conn.).

I should like to express my special thanks to Gale Pedrick, Esq., who as owner of the copyright of *Recollections of Dante Gabrielle Rossetti and his Circle* by Henry Treffry Dunn, edited by Gale Pedrick, has been good enough to allow me to quote a long extract from this work. Lady Haggard and Messrs. A. P. Watt & Son have added their very kind permission to that of Messrs. Longmans, Green & Co., Ltd., for me to quote certain passages from *The Days of my Life* by the late Sir H. Rider Haggard. Sir John Alexander Hammerton has been good enough to add his permission to that of Messrs. Samson Low, Marston & Co., Ltd., for quotations from his book *Barrie : The Story of a Genius,* and R. L. Mégroz, Esq., has also given me his personal consent in addition to that of Messrs. Faber & Faber for the use of a quotation from his book, *Dante Gabriel Rossetti.* Clive Holland, Esq., M.B.E., has also given me leave in conjunction with his Publishers, Messrs. Herbert Jenkins, to reprint an extract from his book *Thomas Hardy, O.M., The Man, His Works and the Land of Wessex*. Messrs. James B. Pinker & Son (of Talbot House, Arundel Street, Strand, London) have, on behalf of the executors of the late Joseph Conrad, Esq., been good enough to permit me to quote a passage from *Joseph Conrad : A Personal Record*. Full particulars of these books will be found in the Bibliography.

ROSAMOND E. M. HARDING.

CAMBRIDGE, 1940

Preface to the Second Edition

In the second edition of *An Anatomy of Inspiration* I have carefully revised the quotations and have corrected a few errors. There is no substantial addition to the text; but I have included statements concerning their methods of work by several well-known living authors whose testimony seemed to me to be of particular interest and importance. Especially am I indebted to Mr. George Bernard Shaw and *The Sheffield Daily Telegraph* for permission to reproduce part of a speech given by Mr. Shaw at the Malvern Festival in 1939; and to Mr. Walter de la Mare and Messrs. Faber and Faber, Ltd., for a quotation from *Behold, This Dreamer*. Mr. Siegfried Sassoon and The University of Bristol have been good enough to allow me to include in the new edition of my book some paragraphs from The University of Bristol Arthur Skemp Memorial Lecture *On Poetry*, and Mr. Basil Hogarth and Messrs. John Lane, The Bodley Head, Ltd., have kindly permitted me to quote some passages of great interest from Mr. Hogarth's book *The Technique of Novel Writing*, to which I am greatly indebted. In conclusion I have to thank Miss Louise Morgan and Messrs. Chatto and Windus, Ltd., for some valuable information quoted verbatim from Miss Morgan's book *Writers at Work*; and Mr. C. Pybus for some very helpful suggestions concerning new material.

The value of the book has been greatly enhanced by the contribution of an Appendix *On the Birth of a Poem* by the well-known poet Mr. Robert Nichols, giving a detailed and brilliant analysis of all the stages in the composition of his "Sunrise Poem."

ROSAMOND E. M. HARDING.

Cambridge, 1942.

Preface to the
Reprint of the Second Edition.

I have been asked to allow a reprint of my *Anatomy of Inspiration* and I have decided that the second edition, published by Messrs. W. Heffer and Sons Ltd. in 1942, is the best of the three.

I have been advised to alter this as little as possible, but there are certain places which seem hastily conceived or to need some alteration. Unfortunately, I destroyed the notebook in which I had copied the extracts used to compile the first edition. Complete revision would therefore be difficult and would probably mean recasting the book, which is not possible for me at present.

If I had been writing this book now I should have written it differently. I have made a few minor alterations which however do not change the character of the book.

The quotations from Coleridge's *Biographia Literaria* given on page 10 of my second chapter do not disclose a somnolent state, but the late Sir Leslie Stephen in his article on Coleridge in the *Dictionary of National Biography*, Vol. IV, (London, O.U.P., 1949-50), p. 771, states that ' "Kubla Khan" was actually a dream, and his best poems are all really dreams, or spontaneous reveries. . . . '

With regard to the feeling of possession discussed on page 13, there is a very interesting passage concerning this in Dame Laura Knight's autobiography entitled *The Magic Line* (London: William Kimber, 1965, pp. 28-29).

Those who do not feel as I do that music is a more subtle medium than poetry for expressing delicate shades of feeling may be interested in the following quotation from *The Notebooks of Samuel Taylor Coleridge*, (edited by Kathleen Coburn; London: Routledge & Kegan Paul Ltd., 2 vols., 1957, 1962; vol. 2 Text, entry no. 2035). Coleridge says: '.../O that I had the Language of Music/the power of infinitely varying the expression, and individualizing it even as it is/—My heart plays incessant music/for which I need an outward Interpreter/—words halt over and over again !—and each time—I feel differently, tho' children of one family.'

I have not felt able to check through this book in any detail owing to heavy pressure of musical work, but I should like to thank certain eminent members of Cambridge University who have most generously spared time to assist me in what I have done, and Messrs. W. Heffer & Sons Ltd. for dealing with the business and technical side of this reprint.

ROSAMOND E. M. HARDING

Cambridge, 1965

Contents

CHAPTER IV

THE REALM OF THE IMAGINATION ITSELF HAS ITS TRUTH.

Ribot on the creative imagination—works of art as well as of mechanism subject to a determinism—the novelist led by his characters—the artist as a discoverer—the artist no less than the man of science must go where the truth leads—great art scientific and impersonal—Sir Philip Sidney on the Poet—great artists faithful to the truths of the imagination.

THE NOVEL.

Inspiration essential before a beginning can be made—searching for striking incident—work does not begin immediately after the inspiration—emotion can only be expressed retrospectively—various means of inducing the state of mind favourable to inspiration—types of inspirational nucleus from which a play or a novel is developed—Zola's method of work—Sir Rider Haggard's methods—Edgar Alan Poe on his method—importance of getting into the right mood—author's choice of words—arduous preparations for the composition of a novel—Flaubert—Pater's method of work—how to describe something never seen or experienced: Charlotte Brontë's method.

POETRY.

Poetic faculty not under the immediate control of the will—pause allowed between the inspiration and the actual work—emotion can only be expressed retrospectively—Wordsworth on the composition of poetry—Shelley composing—various types of inspirational nucleus from which a poem is developed—Housman on the origin of his poems—death as a source of inspiration to the poet—poetry inspired by music—the poetic mood—a musical state of mind in a poet—Burns' method of composing poems to ballads—Walt Whitman's method of composition—Edgar Alan Poe and the *Raven*—Goldsmith's method when composing *The Deserted Village*—Browning's method of work as described by W. M. Rossetti. The thought out poem and the 'automatic' poem—what both owe to chance—poetic inspiration must be checked—Voltaire on his way of checking a poem—times of day and seasons of the year most favourable to poetic inspiration—requirements of a poet—possession of the *poetic faculty—negative capability—the poetic character*.

CHAPTER V

MUSIC.

Comparison of music with poetry—music like poetry built up around moods—comparison of music with painting—general procedure in composition analogous to that of the poet when composing—environment suitable for musical composition—pause left between the inspiring impulse and the actual work—Weber composing an opera—Haydn's

method of work—Balakirev composing *King Lear*—
Tchaikovsky's method of composing—musical inspiration
must be checked—Elgar's method of work when composing
The Apostles—music the outcome of varying moods—circumstances and objects giving rise to musical inspiration—
the effect on the musician of words—of Nature—unexpected
effect of Nature on certain musicians—cheerful music not
necessarily the outcome of a cheerful mood—Beethoven's
love of Nature—the musical mind sensitive to any superficial likeness to printed notes in the objects around him—for
example Weber's march in *Oberon*.

PAINTING.

Painters may be divided into two main groups: (1) poet-
painters, (2) scientist-painters—to poet-painters art is never
an exact copying of Nature—poet-painters and their
methods — Turner — Gainsborough — Corot — Millet —
Whistler—Van Gogh—procedure of poet-painters summarised—scientist-painters object to make an exact representation of some phase of Nature—Ruskin—Constable—
Sargent — Monet — procedure of scientist-painters summarised.—Portrait-painting—Sir Joshua Reynolds' advice concerning first thoughts in art—accident—Blake's
warning.

SCIENTIFIC RESEARCH.

The role of 'feeling' or intuition in scientific research—
no one a good observer unless a good theoriser—noting ex-
emptions—teaching combined with research—thinking
without the use of words—using nonsense words as
temporary symbols—Darwin's method of note-taking.

CHAPTER VI

CHAPTER I

PREPARATION

'Let poets dream, let artists dream, let philosophers
dream : let all thinkers be dreamers,' said Victor Hugo.[152]*
In fact all creative thinkers are dreamers.   In the older
biographies and letters this faculty is often referred to as
'castle-building' or 'day-dreaming.'   Herbert Spencer, in his
Autobiography, tells us that when he was a boy he 'was much
given to castle-building' and that this led to the intense
concentration of his later years.   'You cannot imagine all
I dream of in my strolls out in the sun,' writes George Sand
to the Countess d'Agoult: . . . 'I recollect having during
whole hours fancied I was wandering through the Alps or in
some part of America.'[275]   'My life,' said Sir Walter Scott,
'though not without its fits of waking and strong exertion,
has been a sort of dream, spent in "chewing the cud of sweet
and bitter fancy" . . . .   Somewhere it is said that this castle-
building . . . is fatal to exertion in actual life.   I cannot tell,
I have not found it so.   I cannot, indeed, say like Madame
de Genlis, that in the imaginary scenes in which I have
acted a part I ever prepared myself for anything which
actually befell me ; but I have certainly fashioned out much
that made the present hour pass pleasantly away, and much
that has enabled me to contribute to the amusement of the
public . . . .[280]   But dreaming will not achieve results by itself.   In the man or woman of genius there are always
present great technical skill and originality.   The technical
skill is sometimes built up from childhood.   The poet may
scribble verses as a child: Landor, for example, from his
earliest school-days, wrote verses for his own amusement,
both in Latin and in English.   'A man may be born a poet,'
writes Siegfried Sassoon, 'but he has to make himself an
artist as well.   He must master the instrument . . . . without
clarified construction and technical control, no poetical
communication can be effective.'[277A]   Millais trained his
memory from boyhood so that after coming in from a walk

* The numbers in the text refer to the Bibliography.

I

he could draw an exact likeness of almost everyone he had
met.[214]   Stevenson tells us that even as a boy when he
went for a walk his mind was busy fitting what he saw with
appropriate words and that when he read a book or a
passage that pleased him he would try to imitate the quality
that had attracted him.[6]   Somerset Maugham used in early
days to 'copy out passages from Dryden, Swift, Addison, and
Cardinal Newman, not so much with any intention of
reproducing them mechanically, as with the intention of
cultivating an ear for the sounds of beautiful prose.'[147B]

A prodigious memory might be thought essential to the
creative mind.   But there have been two men at least who
reached eminence whose memories were perhaps only a
little above the average.   Priestley openly confessed to a
defective memory and tells us in his *Memoirs* that he 'had
to devise, and have recourse to, a variety of mechanical
expedients to secure and arrange' his thoughts.[252] Darwin
said 'my memory is extensive, yet hazy' and that he could
not remember for more than a few days a date or line of
poetry.[67] A vast memory is not, in fact, essential.   Systematic and careful note-taking and the use of indexes may
supply the deficiency.
    The power of reading with great rapidity is sometimes
cultivated : for example, Edison, the inventor, could read a
book line by line.[89]   Shelley took in seven or eight lines of
print at a time.[206]   Thackeray would run his eye down the
page and turn over to the next ; assimilating the contents at
a glance.[328] Southey could see at once if the page contained
anything of interest to him.[292]   Schopenhauer, on the other
hand, tended to discourage reading because he thought that
the assimilation of so many new ideas checked the flow of
original thought.[365] Byron evidently thought much the same
for he once remarked to Lady Blessington 'to be perfectly
original one should think much and read little,' but he
qualifies this statement by adding 'and this is impossible,
for one must have read much before one learns to think ;

for I have no faith in innate ideas, whatever I may have in innate predispositions. . . .'[23]

Originality depends on new and striking combinations of ideas. It is obvious therefore that the more a man knows the greater scope he has for arriving at striking combinations. And not only the more he knows about his own subject but *the more he knows beyond it of other subjects.* It is a fact that has not yet been sufficiently stressed that some persons who have risen to eminence in arts, letters or sciences have occasionally possessed considerable knowledge of subjects outside their own sphere of activity. There is a letter in which Pasteur reminds his father that his researches on molecular dissymmetry of natural organic products with their epoch-making results, were founded 'on various notions borrowed from *diverse branches* of science.'[224] What kind of knowledge and interests has a great scientist? Pasteur was a bachelor of literature as well as a doctor of science and his knowledge included crystallography, physics and chemistry. Lamarck began his career as a soldier, became a botanist and professor of invertebrate zoology; he also read physics, chemistry, meteorology and geography. Dr. Priestley's son speaks of the variety of his father's knowledge and of his miscellaneous reading as being 'at all times very extensive.'[253] Herbert Spencer's Papers cover a range of subjects, as he tells us 'from State-functions to a levelling-staff; from the genesis of religious ideas to a watch escapement; from the circulation in plants to an invalid bed; from the law of organic symmetry to planing machinery; from principles of ethics to a velocimeter; from a metaphysical doctrine to a binding-pin; from a classification of the sciences to an improved fishing-rod joint; from the general Law of Evolution to a better mode of dressing artificial flies.'[294]

It would be an interesting experiment to set a series of questions for school children asking them to state what they would consider to be the likely interests and hobbies of certain famous men and women. It is doubtful if they would guess, for example, at the extensive and varied culture of James Watt, who, in addition to his knowledge of

mechanics, was a skilled chemist and versed in most branches
of physical science. He was interested in antiquities,
metaphysics, medicine, etymology, music and law, and he
knew German well enough to read the works of the German
philosophers and to discuss modern German poetry.[223]
Emmanuel Kant read classics, mathematics, physics,
astronomy, metaphysics, law, geography, travel, etc.[306]
Amongst the older books in his library of about 500 volumes,
works on physics and mathematics predominated over
works of philosophy.[307]   Once he described Westminster Bridge to an English acquaintance in such detail that
he was asked how many years he had lived in London
—Kant had never visited England in his life![305] Goethe's
studies and interests were extensive.   He was a great
collector of objects of art and of science.   In his house
there were collections of 'engravings, etchings, drawings,
autographs, coins, medals, plaques, majolicas, plaster casts,
minerals, plants, fossils (about 4000), skeletons.'[16]   He
watched the fields of art, literature and science at Berlin,
Vienna, Munich, Paris, Milan, London and Edinburgh. He
was interested in the construction of canals, harbours and
tunnels.   He followed with close attention the Greek war
of liberty and took in periodicals of all the great European
countries.[17]   Turning now to writers of novels we pick at
random two : George Eliot and Alphonse Daudet.   Philology
was George Eliot's favourite subject of study.   In addition
to this she read vastly not only serious works but novels
such as those by Cherbuliez, Daudet, Gustave Droz and
George Sand.   She had a complete literary and scholarly
knowledge of French, German, Italian and Spanish, and
she read both Greek and Latin for pleasure.   Hebrew was
a favourite study to the end, and she was interested, though
not learned, in astronomy.[65]   Léon Daudet says of his father
Alphonse : 'His knowledge was vast and accurate.   Moreover he surprised me sometimes, when our talk fell upon
some scientific or social subject, by the truth of his information. . . .   He read enormously and with method, and
assimilated difficult questions to his mind with marvellous
quickness.'[69]

Sir Francis Galton, in a well-known passage, says that 'the successful progress of thought appears to depend— first, on a large attendance in the antechamber [of consciousness] : secondly, on the presence there of no ideas except such as are strictly germane to the topic under consideration ; thirdly, on the justness of the logical mechanism that issues the summons.'[106] Success depends on adequate knowledge : that is, it depends on sufficient knowledge of the special subject, and a variety of extraneous knowledge to produce new and original combinations of ideas. Technical skill must be so far developed that it is never a hindrance to the flow of ideas. The thinker does not sit down and say to himself : 'now I am going to think out the relations between so and so.' The process is not so much an active as a passive one. In short the thinker dreams over his subject. The success of this meditation depends, as Sir Francis Galton says, on the absence of irrelevant ideas. In order to inhibit irrelevant ideas the dreaming must be combined with a certain intensity of feeling.

The ideas connected with a favourite study appear to acquire a certain tone which binds them together as an interest, so that when the thinker gets into the mood associated with this subject all relevant ideas in any way connected with it will tend to come together or at any rate to become available. On the other hand the mood tends to act as a sieve which prevents the entry of irrelevant ideas, allowing only those which are relevant to enter. Galton himself says that the 'exclusion of alien ideas is accompanied by a sense of mental effort and volition whenever the topic under consideration is unattractive, otherwise it proceeds automatically, for if an intruding idea finds nothing to cling to, it is unable to hold its place . . .'[106] It has been suggested that many ideas outside the subject become associated with it by a kind of interest association and acquire a similar tone. Thus they tend to become available at the same time as the ideas directly connected with the subject itself.[142] The variety of interests tends to increase the richness of these extra ideas—fringe-ideas—associated with the subject and thus to increase the possibilities of new and original combinations of thought.

Dreaming over a subject is simply the faculty of allowing the will to focus the mind passively on the subject so that it follows the trains of thought as they arise, stopping them only when unprofitable, but in general allowing them to form and branch naturally until some useful or interesting results occur.   Having learned to dream over the subject the thinker must learn not to obtrude his own personal wishes but to follow where the truth leads.   He who wishes to express *himself* is on the wrong track : his aim should be to express beyond himself.   In fact the procedure bears an analogy to the mystic way.   The sinking of the personality ; the retirement for the time-being of the intellect from everything irrelevant ; holding the intellect by the will so that it watches, but does not disturb, the natural development of the idea ; merging himself into the great sea of life beyond himself in order that he may become one with it : these are the characteristics alike of mystic, seer, and thinker.   Hugo said : 'One must fill oneself with human science.   Above all and in spite of all, be a man.'   'Do not fear to surcharge yourself with humanity.   Ballast your mind with reality and then throw yourself into the sea. The sea is inspiration.'[152]

CHAPTER II

THE APPEARANCE OF INSPIRATION

'We are of nature, in nature, by nature, and for nature. Talent, will, genius, are natural phenomena like the lake, the volcano, the mountain, the wind, the star, the cloud.'[203] In these words George Sand makes it clear that the phenomena of creative thought is a natural process. We may add natural in the same way as the experiences of mystics are natural: so rare in their extreme form as to appear supernatural and so common in their lesser manifestations as to pass almost unnoticed. The processes of creative thought which include, in the cases we shall review, inspiration, are best explained in the words of those who possessed the creative faculty in its highest form. The letters of Tchaikovsky are particularly suitable for this purpose as he analyses his own creative process in great detail. From one of these letters addressed to his intimate friend Frau von Meck, we shall draw throughout this chapter. That it should be the letter of a musician does not matter since the main principles of the creative process are the same whatever the subject may be. Tchaikovsky writes: 'generally speaking, the germ of a future composition comes suddenly and unexpectedly.'[316] Now the suddenness with which an idea of value makes its appearance is a characteristic not only of musical thought but also of every type of creative mind. For example, Alfred Russel Wallace would be disinclined to work for days and even for weeks, feeling no constraining impulse. He occupied himself with his seeds, by planning a new house or simply with a novel. Then, 'suddenly whilst in one of his day-dreams, or in a fever (as at Ternate . . .)' James Marchant tells us that 'an explanation, a theory, a discovery, the plan of a new book, came to him like a flash of light,' and with it not only the plan but the material, arguments and illustrations.[197] George Eliot, in a letter to Blackwood of January, 1861, says: 'I am writing a story which came *across* my other plans by a sudden inspiration.'[63] Vincent van Gogh once said that he had 'a terrible lucidity at

7

moments, when nature is so glorious in those days I am hardly conscious of myself and the picture comes to me like in a dream.'[116]   Thomas Hardy 'recalled how, when wandering about the countryside, ideas often came into his head when he had not a scrap of paper upon him. Under such conditions he said that he would pick up large dead leaves, chips of wood left by the woodmen, or pieces of slate, and jot down rapidly upon these unusual materials the ideas which came into his head.'[148]

Returning to Tchaikovsky's letter: he says 'if the soil is ready—that is to say, if the disposition for work is there—it' [the germ of a composition] 'takes root with extraordinary force and rapidity, shoots up through the earth, puts forth branches, leaves, and finally blossoms. I cannot,' he says, 'define the creative process in any other way than by this simile. The great difficulty is that the germ must appear at a favourable moment, the rest goes of itself. It would be vain to try to put into words that immeasurable sense of bliss which comes over me directly a new idea awakens in me and begins to assume a definite form. I forget everything and behave like a madman. Everything within me starts pulsing and quivering; hardly have I begun the sketch ere one thought follows another.'[316]

The state of mind that Tchaikovsky is describing is none other than the state of inspiration. The emotion does not necessarily come at once; it may begin gradually: 'the faint conceptions I have of Poems to come brings the blood frequently into my forehead,' said Keats.[167]   William James refers to 'fevered states' when 'ideas are shooting together' and he 'can think of no finite things.' Scott speaks of the pulse rising as ideas come, and when they flag he says 'something like a snow haze covers my whole imagination.'[282] Or it may come as a tremendous shock to the poet 'musing deeply,' as Shelley tells us in the *Hymn to Intellectual Beauty*:

>   'Sudden, thy shadow fell on me;
>   I shrieked, and clasped my hands in ecstasy!'

Henry Treffry Dunn gives an interesting account of Swinburne under the influence of inspiration in Rossetti's studio at Cheyne Walk: 'It had been a very sultry day, and with the advancing twilight heavy thunder-clouds were rolling up.

The door opened and Swinburne entered. He appeared in an abstracted state, and for a few moments sat silent. Soon, something I had said anent his last poem set his thoughts loose. Like the storm that had just broken, so he began in low tones to utter lines of poetry. As the storm increased, he got more and more excited and carried away by the impulse of his thoughts, bursting into a torrent of splendid verse that seemed like some grand air with the distant peals of thunder as an intermittent accompaniment. And still the storm waxed more violent, and the vivid flashes of lightning became more frequent. But Swinburne seemed unconscious of it all, and whilst he paced up and down the room, pouring out bursts of passionate declamation, faint electric sparks played round the wavy masses of his luxuriant hair. I lay on the sofa in a corner of the studio and listened in wonder and with a curious awe, for it appeared to me as though the very figures in the pictures that were on the easels standing about the room were conscious of and sympathized with the poet and his outpourings.'[87]

'In the midst of this magic process'—that is, the process of inspiration—Tchaikovsky continues: 'it frequently happens that some external interruption wakes me from my somnambulistic state : a ring at the bell, the entrance of my servant, the striking of the clock, reminding me that it is time to leave off. Dreadful, indeed, are such interruptions. Sometimes they break the thread of inspiration for a considerable time, so that I have to seek it again—often in vain. In such cases cool headwork and technical knowledge have to come to my aid. Even in the works of the greatest master,' he continues, 'we find such moments, when the organic sequence fails and a skilful join has to be made, so that the parts appear as a completely welded whole.'[316] Interruptions are, indeed, a very serious menace to those engaged in creative work. The final lines of *Kubla Khan*, for example, were lost owing to Coleridge's being called out by a 'person on business from Porlock'!

Tchaikovsky refers to his somnambulistic state during which his ideas assume a definite form. Somnolent state would seem a more accurate term ; a condition which Yeats and others describe as being 'both asleep and awake' such that the 'imagination,' as Coleridge says, 'is put in action by the will and understanding and retained under their irremissive, though gentle and unnoticed controul'; a state in which 'judgment [is] ever awake and steady self-possession, with enthusiasm and feeling profound or vehement.'[51]   In other words, the imagination is focussed in some particular direction and is set, as it were, to do its work in that position by the will; the understanding watching the movements with profound attention and pruning away unwanted developments whilst retaining those of value.   There is a letter attributed to Mozart that shows the process very well :* 'when I am, as it were, completely myself, entirely alone, and of good cheer—say, travelling in a carriage, or walking after a good meal, or during the night when I cannot sleep; it is on such occasions that my ideas flow best and most abundantly. . . . Those ideas that please me I retain in memory, and am accustomed, as I have been told, to hum them to myself.   If I continue in this way, it soon occurs to me how I may turn this or that morsel to account so as to make a good dish of it. . . . All this fires my soul, and provided I am not disturbed, my subject enlarges itself, becomes methodised and defined, and the whole, though it be long, stands almost complete and finished in my mind, so that I can survey it, like a fine picture or a beautiful statue at a glance.   Nor do I hear in my imagination the parts *successively*, but I hear them, as it were, all at once. . . . What a delight this is I cannot tell!   All this inventing, this producing, takes place in a pleasing lively dream.'[211]   Wagner discovered the opening of the *Rheingold* during 'half-sleep' on a couch in the Hotel at Spezia[229]; and in a letter to Frau Wesendonck he refers to the blissful dream-state into which he falls when composing.[230]   A new version of the Symphony No. 3 in C came to Sir Hubert Parry quite suddenly as he lay trying to sleep on the afternoon of 21st September, 1888.[123]   Debussy once said 'there are moments when I lose the feeling of things around me. . . .'[183]   Dr. W. H. Rivers, the

* See *Allgemeine musikalische Zeitung* (Leipzig), 23 August, 1815. (Siebzehnter Jahrgang.) No. 34. S.561 bis 566. Jahn considers this letter to be a fabrication.   See *The Life of Mozart*, trans. by P. D. Townsend.   3 vols.   London: Novello, Ewer & Co.   1882.   Vol. 2, p. 415, *note* 6.

well-known psychologist, stated that many of the scientific ideas he valued most, as well as the language in which they were expressed, came to him in the 'half-sleeping half-waking state directly continuous with definite sleep.'[271] This half-sleep is so common with poets that it scarcely requires comment. Wordsworth told Bonamy Price that the line in his *Ode*, beginning 'Fallings from us, vanishings' which has since puzzled so many readers, refers to those trance-like states to which he was at one time subject. During these moments the world around him seemed unreal and the Poet had occasionally to use his strength against an object such as a gate-post, to reassure himself.[239] There is a very interesting reference to this trance-like condition by W. B. Yeats in his Essay, *Symbolism of Poetry*, where he tells us that on one occasion when he was writing a highly symbolic and abstract poem, his pen fell to the ground. As he stooped to pick it up he began to remember some fantastic adventure and then another until he realised that he was remembering his dreams for many nights. He then tried to recall what he had done that morning, but his waking life, he tells us, had perished from his mind ; and it was only after a struggle that he came to remember it again. He says 'had my pen not fallen on the ground and so made me turn from the images that I was weaving into verse, I would never have known that meditation had become trance. . . . So I think that in the making and in the understanding of a work of art . . . we are lured to the threshold of sleep, and it may be far beyond it, without knowing that we have ever set our feet upon the steps of horn or of ivory.'[362] Shelley, in his poem *Mont Blanc*, gives another instance of this dreamy trance-like condition when the mind of the poet purified of all irrelevant matters :

> '. . . passively
> Now renders and receives fast influencings,
> Holding an unremitting interchange
> With the clear universe of things around;
> One legion of wild thoughts, . . .'

Further on, in the same poem, he asks the question :

> 'Has some unknown omnipotence unfurled
> The veil of life and death? Or do I lie
> In dream, ...'

Inspiration occasionally arises during actual sleep.   Tartini's violin sonata *Trillo del Diavolo* owed its inspiration to a dream in which the composer imagined that the Devil played upon his violin a piece of surpassing beauty and brilliance.[146] The three opening stanzas of *A Vision of Spring in Winter* came to Swinburne during actual sleep.[121] Another example is *Kubla Khan* which came to Coleridge when in a deep sleep caused by an opiate.[53]* Medwin tells us that at one time of his life Shelley made a practice of noting down his dreams.[207] But on the whole, it would seem safe to say that the state when both asleep and awake is the most favourable to inspiration.   In short: it is with the 'eyes of heavy mind' that the creative artist sees his visions.

Tchaikovsky says : 'If that condition of mind and soul, which we call *inspiration*, lasted long without intermission, no artist could survive it.   The strings would break and the instrument be shattered into fragments.   It is already a great thing if the main ideas and general outline of a work come without any racking of brains, as the result of that supernatural and inexplicable force we call inspiration.'[316] 'The mind in creation,' says Shelley, 'is as a fading coal, which some invisible influence, like an inconstant wind, awakens to transitory brightness ; this power arises from within. . . . Could this influence be durable in its original purity and force it is impossible to predict the greatness of the results ; but when composition begins, inspiration is already on the decline. . . . .'[286]

There is a curious phenomenon that may be noted in passing.   In that phase of inspiration when, as James says, 'ideas are shooting together,' the mind occasionally presents ideas in unexpected order, or ideas that belong elsewhere— a kind of double inspiration. William Reed notes that often ideas would come to Elgar that had nothing to do with the work he had then in hand.   He used to note them down and find a place for them later or in another work.[260] Rimsky-Korsakoff, speaking of his *Christmas Eve*, states that 'the

---

* See Lombroso (Cesare), *The Man of Genius.*   London: Walter Scott, 1891, pp. 21-22, where further examples of inspiration occurring during dreams are given.

writing of *Christmas Eve* held first place with me ; yet even at that time there came into my head some new musical ideas for *Sadko.* ...'[270] When Berlioz was composing his Trio *Ange Adoré*, he was surprised sometimes by the unexpected order in which his ideas came to him.[343] Thackeray's daughter, Anne Ritchie, in her Preface to *The Newcomes*, shows that ideas for this novel were already coming into Thackeray's mind while he was still working on *Esmond*. She says : 'The story (i.e. *The Newcomes*) had been in his mind for a long time. While still writing "Esmond" he speaks of a new novel "opening with something like Fareham and the old people there," and of "a hero who will be born in India, and have a half-brother and sister".'[324]

The state of inspiration is often accompanied by two distinct and vivid impressions ; the sense of possession and the sense of compulsion. The sense of being possessed and used as a mouthpiece is, of course, a frequent experience of saints and mystics who from the very nature of their vocation would expect to be the channels of divine light. Thus St. Catherine of Sienna, speaking of the power of writing she had received miraculously from God, says : 'In a wondrous way, He set it for me in my mind, even as the master does to the child when he gives him the copy.'[108] The great German mystic Jakob Boehme, speaking of the inspired writing which followed after his seven years of silence, tells us that 'Art has not wrote here . . . but all was ordered according to the Direction of the Spirit. ...'[24] And to take one more instance, Madame Guyon confesses 'Before writing I did not know what I was going to write ; while writing I saw that I was writing things I had never known. ...'[129] In fact, writers of automatic script, whether religious or secular in character, are certain that they are being operated by some other power. It does not appear, however, to be so widely recognised and known that the great creative thinkers who are not professed religious : musicians, novelists as well as poets, and scientists also, are often surprised to astonishment at the results of their work which seems to have been in some way 'given' to them.

Fantastic as this statement may at first appear, there is ample testimony to support it.

Blake, referring to his poem *Milton*, in a letter to Thomas Butts, says, 'I have written this poem from immediate dictation, twelve or sometimes twenty or thirty lines at a time, without premeditation, and even against my will.'[20] Goethe looked upon his genius as a mysterious power; his poems came to him of themselves and at times even against his will. 'The songs made me,' he said, 'not I them; the songs had me in their power.'[12] The description of Apollo in the third book of Hyperion seemed to Keats to have come 'by chance or magic—to be as it were something given to him.' He said also that he had often 'not been aware of the beauty of some thought or expression until after he had composed and written it down. It has then struck him with astonishment and seemed rather the production of another person than his own.'[187] Sidney Dobell, the poet, in a letter to George Gilfillan, says 'whenever I write the feeling of being a *receiver*, an instrument, a *mouthpiece*, has always been so strong on me that I should as soon have accompanied a draught from our hill streams with the chip of the rock it ran through as have associated—when offering you a poem—the thought with a portrait of the thinker. . . .'[162] George Eliot told J. W. Cross 'that, in all that she considered her best writing, there was a "not herself" which took possession of her, and that she felt her own personality to be merely the instrument through which this spirit, as it were, was acting.' This was the case especially in *Middlemarch* in the scene when Dorothea is in Rosamond's drawing-room, when she felt herself entirely possessed by the feelings of the two women.[65] George Sand declares: 'My being is essentially a passive being, and I am not *quite* responsible for my productions, good or bad. They are, probably, the result of previous reflections or impressions; but they are not the immediate outcome of my will.'[276] In a letter to Flaubert she says: 'the wind plays my old harp as it lists. It has its *high notes*, its *low notes*, its heavy notes— and its faltering notes, in the end it is all the same to me provided the emotion comes, but I can find nothing in myself. It is *the other* who sings as he likes, well or ill, and when I try to think about it, I am afraid and tell myself that I am nothing, nothing at all.'

'But a great wisdom saves us; we know how to say to ourselves, "Well, even if we are absolutely nothing but instruments, it is still a charming state and like no other, this feeling oneself vibrate".'[200]

Dickens declared that when he sat down to his book 'some beneficent power' showed it all to him.[100] Thackeray says in *The Round-about Papers* 'I have been surprised at the observations made by some of my characters. It seems as if an occult Power was moving the pen. The personage does or says something, and I ask, how the dickens did he come to think of that?' And after referring to the unforeseen and strange utterances of the personages met with in dreams he says: 'In like manner, the imagination foretells things. We spake anon of the inflated style of some writers. What also if there is an *afflated* style,—when a writer is like a Pythoness on her oracle tripod and mighty words, words he cannot help, come blowing, and bellowing, and whistling, and moaning through the speaking pipes of his bodily organ?'[331] Tchaikovsky tells us how he sketched the whole of the *Tempest* overture as if he were possessed by some supernatural force. Parry refers to 'exaltation [that] is so great that the vitality becomes almost supernatural.'[125] Elgar looked upon himself as the 'all but unconscious medium' by which his works had come into being.[192] Reference will be made in due course to the extraordinary powers of intuition of Lord Kelvin, of Einstein, and of the inventor Edison. 'I have long since come to see,' declared Alfred Russel Wallace, 'that no one deserves either praise or blame for the *ideas* that come to him, but only for the actions resulting therefrom. Ideas and beliefs are certainly not voluntary acts. They come to us—we hardly know *how* or *whence* . . . .'[196]

With the sense of possession goes also the feeling of compulsion. 'William wished to break off composition, but was unable, and so did himself harm,' records Dorothy Wordsworth.[359A] Thackeray said 'when I am in labour with a book I don't quite know what happens, I sit for hours before my paper, not doing my book, but incapable of doing

anything else, and thinking upon that subject always, waking
with it, walking about with it, and going to bed with it.'[329]
Forster alludes to the strange mastery that *A Christmas Carol*
had over Dickens, 'how he wept over it, and laughed, and
wept again, and excited himself to an extraordinary degree,
and how he walked thinking of it fifteen and twenty miles
about the black streets of London' when most people were
in bed.[97]   When George Meredith had once begun a story
the characters took possession of him and developed into an
influence on his life.   He would work for hours during the
day and even late at night stopping only for Cole the
gardener to bring his meals.[283]   Schopenhauer said 'If I
faintly perceive an idea which looks like a dim picture before
me, I am possessed with an ineffable longing to grasp it ; I
leave everything else, and follow my idea through all its
tortuous windings, as the huntsman follows the stag.'[364]

Many are the stories told of the absorption and absence of
mind of men and women of genius when 'compelled' by an
idea.   Jules Sandeau once called on Balzac and spoke to
him of his sister's illness.   Balzac listened absently for a
time, then losing patience interrupted him with 'All that,
my friend, is very well, but let us come back to reality ; let
us speak of *Eugénie Grandet*.'[175]   Sir Walter Scott was
remarkable for his absorption and its consequent result,
absence of mind.   He had an old Aunt, a Mrs. Curle, on
whom he used to call whenever he visited Jedburgh.   The
old lady had removed to another house and although Sir
Walter knew this, old habit led him to her former residence.
Despite the fact that the lady who now occupied the house
was thin and shrivelled, while Mrs. Curle was stout and
burly-looking, Scott showed no surprise when he saw her
but said 'How do you do my dear Aunt'? and at once proceeded to embrace her![288]

The creative process is sometimes accompanied with restlessness ; and especially was this the case with Dickens who
speaks of the 'restlessness and waywardness of an author's
mind,'[74] and in another place he says 'I am settling to work
again, and my horrible restlessness immediately assails me.
It belongs to such times.'[76]   Creation is not, in fact, always

and at all times a pleasant process. On the one hand periods of compulsion and feverish output :—The immense speed of work of Handel and Mozart : Handel composing the Messiah in five weeks ; Pascal writing his Treatise on the Cycloid in one week[244] ; Balzac composing *La Cousine Bette* in six weeks[94] ; Mark Twain writing, as he tells us, at one time 'an average of 3,000 words a day'[348] ; and Sir Rider Haggard composing *She* at 'white heat' in a little over six weeks.[131] To balance this we have on the other hand, Thackeray moaning about the hours he had spent over two pages[92] ; Dostoevsky exclaiming that he simply didn't 'know how anyone can write at great speed and only for money's sake'[83] ; Adam Smith declaring after a life-time of writing he 'composed as slowly, and with as great difficulty as at first'[301] ; and Beethoven writing and re-writing a dozen times almost every bar of his music.[128] The creative process brings with it as many pains as joys. As in the case of religious mystics we read of periods of dryness: 'William tired himself with hammering at a passage,' writes Dorothy Wordsworth in her *Journal*.[359B] 'Inspiration will not come,' says Tchaikovsky; 'every day I begin something and lose heart'; and again, 'grey, without inspiration or joy.'[320] When Parry was composing *Judith* there were times when he was 'stuck fast in a chorus' and 'having to smite it out bit by bit.'[122] George Eliot was particularly subject to these periods of depression, for instance in her diary at the time of composing *Romola* are found such entries as these : 'got into a state of so much wretchedness in attempting to concentrate my thoughts on the construction of my story, that I became desperate, and suddenly burst my bonds, saying, I will not think of writing!' and again later, 'still with an incapable head—trying to write, trying to construct, and unable.'[64] Flaubert writes to George Sand, 'As for my frenzy for work, I will compare it to an attack of herpes. I scratch myself while I cry. It is both a pleasure and a torture at the same time. And I am doing nothing that I want to! For one does not choose one's subjects, they force themselves on one.'[202] Joseph Conrad speaking of *Nostromo* says 'All I know, is that, for twenty months neglecting the common joys of life that fall to the lot of

the humblest on this earth, I had, like the prophet of old,
"wrestled with the Lord" for my creation' . . .; and later
he speaks of the 'strain of a creative effort in which mind
and will and conscience are engaged to the full, hour after
hour, day after day. . . .'[58]   Turning now to a musician:
George Sand after describing Chopin's creation as miraculous
and coming on his piano suddenly, complete, or singing in
his head during a walk; says that afterwards 'began the most
heart-rending labour I ever saw.   It was a series of efforts,
of irresolutions, and of frettings to seize again certain details
of the theme he had heard'; he would 'shut himself up in his
room for whole days, weeping, walking, breaking his pens,
repeating and altering a bar a hundred times,' and spending
six weeks over a single page to write it at last as he had noted
it down at the very first.[234]   It is related of Delacroix that
often before he began a painting he experienced those
languors 'reluctances and agitations that recall the Pytheness
fleeing from the god.'   Nor are philosophers exempt.   When
James was composing his *Principles of Psychology* we are
told that the periods of outpourings alternated with periods
of 'painful effort.'

The whole appearance and manner of the Pytheness
underwent a change when exhausted with her struggles she
finally sank beneath the power of the God.   Something very
like this happens when the creative process is at its height.
Eye-witnesses have left descriptions of what they saw.
Anton Schindler shall describe what Beethoven looked like
when in his 'raptus.'   Beethoven, as is known, was not remarkable in appearance; he was short and thick-set; his
eyes were small and were almost hidden when he laughed.
'On the other hand,' Schindler says, 'they would suddenly be
projected in unusual size, flashing as they rolled about, the
pupils almost always turned upward, or immovable, staring
down before them as soon as some idea had seized him.
Therewith, however, his whole outward appearance would in
the same way suddenly undergo a startling transformation,
would assume a vividly inspired and imposing semblance,
so that his slight figure, like his soul, would tower before one
in gigantic size.   These moments of sudden inspiration often

would surprise him in the midst of the gayest company or in the street, and usually attracted the liveliest attention of all passers-by.'[8] Mozart, also, was unimpressive in appearance, yet in moments of inspiration the artist within him became apparent in the mysterious change that came over his countenance.[159] Schubert's friends knew by his 'flashing eye and altered tone of voice when an idea had seized him.'[144] Wagner also had his 'raptus.' Weissheimer tells how once when he disturbed him when composing the *Meistersinger*, Wagner had opened the door and stood before him scarcely recognisable; 'his features were completely changed, almost wild.'[230] Whoever had looked into Wagner's eyes would be unlikely to forget their mysterious expression.[231] This changed appearance is not confined only to musicians. Medwin says of Shelley when inspired: 'his eyes flashed, his lips quivered, his voice was tremulous with emotion, a sort of ecstasy came over him, and he talked more like a spirit or an angel than a human being.[205] D'Israeli tells an amusing·story of the poet Gray when composing the 'Installation Ode':—'A friend calling on him, Gray flung open his door hastily, and in a hurried voice and tone exclaiming, in the first verse of that Ode,

"Hence, avaunt! 'tis holy ground!"—

his friend started back at the disordered appearance of the bard, whose organism had disturbed his very air and countenance, till he had recovered himself.'[79] Mrs. Gaskell observed that Charlotte Brontë had peculiar eyes, 'large and well shaped ; their colour a reddish brown. . . . The usual expression was of quiet listening intelligence ; but now and then, on some just occasion for vivid interest or wholesome indignation, a light would shine out, as if some spiritual lamp had been kindled. . . . I never saw the like in any other human creature.'[109]

How wise was George Sand to warn us that genius is natural! Sir Joshua Reynolds said 'it is very natural for those who are unacquainted with the *cause* of anything extraordinary, to be astonished at the *effect*, and to consider it as a kind of magick.'[262] Some men of genius were indeed offended by the term inspiration. Constable was one of

these.   When Blake, looking at one of his studies of fir
trees, exclaimed, 'Why this is not drawing, but *inspiration.*'
Constable replied: 'I never knew it before; I meant it for
drawing.'[180]   Rodin warns us against inspired moments
that 'by inducing a condition akin to intoxication, may
cause the artist to forget the very principles on which the
adequate interpretation of his idea most certainly depends.'[190]
Gustave Flaubert wrote that 'you should mistrust everything which resembles inspiration, for that is often nothing
more than a deliberate determination and forced excitement,
voluntarily caused, and which did not come of itself;
besides,' he continues, 'we do not live in inspiration;
Pegasus walks more often than he gallops, genius consists in
showing how to make him take the pace we require. . . .'[312]

Chapter III

GENERAL PROCEDURE

The idea coming suddenly into the mind with the glow of inspiration must be noted down before it fades or is lost. When Corot, the landscape-painter, had some new conception it was his custom to adapt it to one of his existing studies in order to save time. The sketches were placed side by side on the floor from one end of his studio to the other ; then Corot chose from them the sketch most suitable for his new atmospherical effect or whatever it might be. He began to paint at once without scraping or preparing the canvas in any way because delay, he said, would give his conception time to evaporate.[19] A fleeting effect of colour or of light and shade may easily be forgotten if it is not put down at once, and in the same way, however strange this may seem, a poem, a sentence, an idea, coming at the time with vivid clarity is lost unless it is noted down at once. A note-book of some sort is, in fact, essential. Rossetti had pockets in his painting coat large enough to hold a good-sized memorandum-book so that he could note down his thoughts for poetry or painting.[86] Rimsky-Korsakoff, when he began his opera *Snyegoorochka* (Snow-maiden), bought a large music-book and wrote down in this the themes and motives as they came into his mind.[269] Rather than run the risk of losing some new aspect of character or development of plot, Thacheray sometimes kept his carriage standing at the door for two hours.[330] Palgrave, speaking of Tennyson, said that if a lyric occurred to Tennyson and 'he did not write it down on the spot, the lyric fled from him irrevocably.'[323] Poets have even left their beds in the middle of the night, as Swinburne did rather than allow some vivid impression to fade away.

The idea springing up suddenly and unexpectedly when, perhaps, the mind is meditating something else, usually brings with it the sense of value. Palgrave suggests that doubtless motives a few bars long came to Mozart and to Beethoven as they did to Tennyson, 'bringing with them a kind of inward assurance that, if seized and worked out, some "treasure for ever" of an air lay concealed behind them.'[323] This is undoubtedly true; Beethoven always carried his note-book with him and Mozart kept music-paper in his coach. And how important these ideas appear is shown by the statement of Tchaikovsky that after the glow of inspiration had come he knew beforehand whatever he wrote that day would have 'power to make an impression and to touch the hearts' of those who heard it.[317]   Nor is it only musical and poetical ideas that coming suddenly and spontaneously carry conviction with them. Sir Joseph Thomson says, 'It is remarkable that when ideas come in this way they carry conviction with them, and dispose without a struggle ideas which previously had seemed not unsatisfactory.'[335]   Henri Poincaré speaks of the 'absolute certainty which accompanies the inspiration,' but he then adds this important warning :

'It is necessary to work out the results of the inspiration . . . to verify them. I have spoken of the feeling of absolute certainty which accompanies the inspiration ; in the cases quoted,' he continues, referring to examples of inspiration in his own work, 'this feeling was not deceptive, and more often than not this will be the case. But we must beware of thinking that this is a rule without exceptions. Often the feeling deceives us without being any less distinct on that account, and we only detect it when we attempt to establish the demonstration. I have noticed this fact most notably with regard to ideas that have come to me in the morning or at night when I have been in bed in a semi-somnolent condition.'[250]   Inspiration should always be verified and, in fact, there are not many thinkers who do not revise and check with care. Louis Pasteur wrote : 'The boldest conceptions, the most legitimate speculations can be embodied but from the day when they are consecrated by observation and experiment.'[344]   Tchaikovsky writes to Frau von Meck : 'What has been set down in a moment of ardour must now be critically examined, improved, extended, or condensed as the form requires.'[319]   Burns said that he composed hastily but corrected at leisure. Samuel Rogers told Dyce that during his whole life he had borne in mind 'the speech of a woman to Philip of Macedon—"I appeal from Philip drunk to Philip sober." After writing anything in the excitement of the moment, and being greatly pleased with it, I have always put it by for a time, and then, carefully considering it in every possible light, I have altered it to the best of my judgment.'[42] George Sand, on the other hand, wrote for hours without pause or erasure, and sent her manuscript to the printer without even reading it through. Once, it is said, having finished a novel at 12 o'clock she put it into an envelope for the printer and, at once, began another novel.[277] But exceptions may be found for every rule, and George Sand's procedure is most unusual if not unique.

The inspiration having been noted down and checked, there are two methods of procedure which may be followed. The one that is chosen depends mostly on the temperament of the thinker. He may be the type to work at one subject only and to become wholly absorbed by it to the exclusion for the time being of everything else or he may prefer to work at several subjects more or less simultaneously. We shall begin with the one-subject procedure. It is simply this : the practice of continuity of attention. Being entirely absorbed in the work ; waking with it, walking with it and sleeping on it until it is completed. Sir William Hamilton said 'the greater capacity of continuous thinking that a man possesses, the longer and more steadily can he follow out the same train of thought,—the stronger is his power of attention ; and in proportion to his power of attention will be the success with which his labour is rewarded.'[135] Newton, Hamilton states, replied to some compliment upon his genius that if he had made any discoveries 'it was owing more to patient attention than to any other talent.' And in much the same words, Hamilton continues, he once heard Mrs. Siddons declare that her superior talent was due to the 'intense study which she bestowed on her parts.' Amongst those whom Sir William quotes as examples of men in whom continuity of attention was a marked characteristic, are Socrates, Descartes, Buffon, Archimedes, Scaliger, and Carneades.[136] It may be of interest to supplement this list with a few names belonging to more recent times. Dugald

Stewart declares that Adam Smith, even when he was with his friends, 'was apt to be engrossed with his studies ; and appeared at times, by the motion of his lips, as well as by his looks and gestures to be in the fervour of composition.'[302] Of Mozart, we know from his sister-in-law, Sophie, that even when he was conversing he appeared to be deeply engrossed with other thoughts.[156] Jean-François Millet, when thinking out his scenes from the legend of St. Geneviève would sit at the table long after meals were done, 'fixing his eyes on the cloth, and passing his finger over the surface as if he were drawing, and then moving his hand as if to rub out what he had drawn.'[40] Burne-Jones, like Mozart, was often seen to be deeply engrossed with other thoughts whilst pleasantly conversing with his wife and friends. When an occasional wrong reply betrayed him he would own up amidst general laughter.[29] Scott's eyes were 'constantly fixed on the ground and he would frequently pause for a minute or two in complete abstraction of mind.'[1] Dickens, writing to a friend, said 'You know my state of mind as well as I do. . . . How I work, how I walk, how I shut myself up, how I roll down hills and climb up cliffs; how the new story is everywhere—heaving in the sea, flying with the clouds, blowing in the wind. . . .'[75] Macaulay once said 'I never write to please myself until my subject has for the time driven every other out of my head.'[342] Landor reproaches Southey : 'How you can write two poems at a time I cannot conceive. I could write history and poetry, but I could not divide my passions and affections. When I write a poem, my heart and all my feelings are upon it. I never commit adultery with another ; and high poems will not admit flirtation.'[101] Isaac D'Israeli declared that 'a continuity of attention, a patient quietness of mind, forms one of the characteristics of genius.'[78]

We have seen how the poet Rogers put away his work for a time. He did not begin to revise it at once or even within a few hours ; he did not become absorbed in it but set it aside to revise at some future time when at leisure. This brings us to a practice which possibly would have surprised Sir William Hamilton, since it is the reverse of that which is described above : the practice of laying aside a work or an idea to mature. When a work is roughed in 'put it on one side and revise later' is the gist of this method. It is embodied in Kipling's advice to young writers: 'Read your final draft, and consider faithfully every paragraph, sentence and word, blacking out where requisite. Let it lie by to drain as long as possible. At the end of that time, re-read and you should find that it should bear a second shortening. Finally, read it aloud alone and at leisure. . . . I have had tales by me for three or five years which shortened themselves almost yearly.'[173]

All the more considerable stories of Stevenson with the exception of *Catriona* were written in two breaks. 'I have to leave off . . . and forget a tale for a little,' Stevenson says, 'then I can return upon it fresh and with interest revived.'[7] Landor once told Southey 'that he could never publish a poem that contained any character of a human being until he had lived two or three years with that character.' . . .[102] W. M. Rossetti said of Browning that he 'often stores-up a subject long before he writes it.'[273] Whittier remembered thinking over the story of *Skipper Ireson* while walking to and fro under Hugh Tallant's sycamores by the river thirty years before he wrote and published that Ballad.[170] The subjects of nearly all Wagner's works were settled more or less definitely, Mr. Newman tells us, at an early stage of his career; but Wagner was obliged to wait for the right psychological moment before he could begin.[228] G. F. Watts usually advised against delay in completing pictures, but in his own case a picture begun 'in the 'fifties might be completed ten, twenty and even thirty years later.'[352]

There is much to be said in favour of laying a work aside to mature; for one thing it gives the judgment time to operate; the mind is able to return to the work from time to time with a fresh outlook; and check it from many different angles. It follows also that if new ideas are to be set aside to develop and newly finished works left to 'mature,' there must be several things on hand at the same time in various stages of development. The continuity of attention is purposely shortened and interrupted partly on account of the rest this gives; Sir Joseph Thomson says that new ideas 'come more freely if the mind does not dwell too long on one subject without interruption'... ,[335] and partly because a change may bring about fruitful combinations of ideas. There is no doubt that it may be an advantage especially in some branches of science to turn from one thing to another, since discoveries may result from an idea from one branch of science being applied to another, as, for example, when electricity began to be used in connection with chemistry.

The practice of keeping several subjects on hand at the same time has had some famous adherents. Henry Cavendish was 'in the constant practice of carrying on together, widely dissimilar enquiries.'[357] Lord Rayleigh always liked to have several things on hand, for if one did not progress he could then turn to another.[255] In the sphere of letters: Jane Austen, at one time, had on hand in various stages, *Sense and Sensibility*, *Pride and Prejudice* and *Mansfield Park*; and again later *Northanger Abbey*, *Sanditon* and *Persuasion*.[266] Southey, Macaulay says, 'would write the *History of Brazil* before breakfast, an ode after breakfast, then the *History of the Peninsular War* till dinner, and an article for the *Quarterly Review* in the evening.'[342] Robert Burns had frequently half-a-dozen or more pieces of different kinds in various stages, turning away from the one, as he tired of it, to the other.[240] Beethoven wrote to Dr. F. Wegeler 'As I am now working I am often engaged on three or four things at the same time.'[10] Watts carried on as many pictures as easels and wall-space allowed; and often, in the same hour, he worked alternatively at five or six, different both in subject and treatment. He found that by working in this manner 'his eye turned with clearer perception from one to another.'[353] Rodin also was in the habit of carrying on a number of different subjects concurrently.[193] Mozart apologises to his sister for sending her a Prelude and Fugue in which the Prelude was inappropriately placed after the Fugue. The reason for this was that he had composed the Fugue first and wrote it down whilst thinking out the Prelude.[157] Alfred de Musset, his brother tells us, would often be dreaming of a poetical subject even while he was writing prose. He considered 'that this twofold exercise of the faculties' was profitable; it was like 'turning your eyes to a more distant star, in order to see more clearly the sparkle of the nearer one.'[226] De Musset has, in fact, pointed out one great advantage of working at two or more subjects at the same time. The mind may become dulled by too long attention to one subject and a change will often enable it to see more clearly than it ever would have done future developments necessary, and any defects there may be in the other work.

A practice that is of great advantage in creative thought is working up the imagination as nearly as possible to the state of vision. To those who are already visualizers this will present no difficulties. Shakespeare, in his Sonnets, has more than one reference to this power in himself. In Sonnet XXIV:

'Mine eye hath play'd the painter and hath stell'd
Thy beautys form in table of my heart;

. . . .

'Mine eyes have drawn thy shape.'

And again, in Sonnet CXIII:

'. . . . mine eye is in my mind.'

Blake told 'his artist friends you have the same faculty as I (the visionary), only you do not trust or cultivate it. You can see what I do, *if you choose.*' On one occasion he said to a young painter, 'You have only to work up imagination to the state of vision and the thing is done.'[114] Northcote declared that 'the painter who has a genius, first makes himself master of the subject he is to represent, by reading or otherwise; then works up his imagination into a kind of enthusiasm, till, in a degree, he perceives the whole event before his eyes, when, quick as lightning, he gives his rough sketch on paper or canvas. By these means his work has the air of genius stamped upon it.'[265] Fantastic as this advice appears there can be no doubt that working up the imagination to the state, or at all events almost to the state, of vision is a practice with certain creative thinkers. Charlotte Brontë must have done something of the kind, for it is known that she attempted at first

to *draw* stories and only upon failure to do this did she turn
to her novel-writing.[112]   Two writers of the present day have
given statements on this subject: Wyndham Lewis and
Siegfried Sassoon.   Wyndham Lewis, when asked by
Louise Morgan if his painting helped him in writing, replied:
'It must of course do that.   The habit of thinking of things
in plastic and pictorial terms must have its influence upon
the writer's art, when you practise both as I do.   First of all,
I *see*!   The first—and last—thing that I do is to use my eyes.
. . . Then the visual discipline began very young.   I began
—yes—with painting: as a small boy I was sent to a London
art school. . . .   All serious writers should be encouraged to
draw and paint—for myself, I suffer a great deal upon those
occasions when I have time to read a few pages of a fellow-
fictionist on account of the *bad drawing* and confused
sentimental and unreal colouring I find in his pages.   The
drawing in some novels is so bad I cannot read them.'[222c]
Siegfried Sassoon, in his "Arthur Skemp Memorial Lecture,"
told his audience: '. . . I have taught myself to write not so
much by the study of verse technicology as by trusting my
own ear. . . .   But the ear is not enough.   There is also
the eye.   Not the eye of the occulist, but the mind's eye;
by which I mean the faculty of inward visualization.'

'I have never been fond of ideas for their own sake.   In
fact they have played a comparatively unimportant part
in my literary life.   My thoughts—if one can call them that
—have been (when allowed to have their own way) a series
of mental pictures.   Thinking in pictures is my natural
method of self-expression.   I have always been a submis-
sively visual writer.' . . .

    ' . . . mind-sight eliminates what is inessential, and
achieves breadth and intensity by transmuted perception.'[277B]

Returning once more to the older writers: Charles Dickens
declared that he *saw* his stories and wrote them down.[100]
Anne Ritchie said that her father Thackeray used to make
notes for his books not only in writing but also with his
brush and pencil.[327]   When Alphonse Daudet was creating he *saw* what he created and when he was writing he
heard.[71]   Shelley 'could throw a veil over his eyes, and
find himself in a *camera obscura*, where all the features

of a scene were reproduced in a form more pure and perfect than they had been originally presented to his external senses.'[206]   Coleridge, in the preface (of 1816) to
his poem 'Christabel,' declares 'I had the whole present to
my mind, with the wholeness no less than the liveliness of a
vision. . . . .'[55] In a letter to Josiah Wedgwood he says 'A
whole essay might be written on the danger of thinking without images'[48]; in another letter to Wedgwood he complains of
the inflammation of his eyes and how he had made some
'curious observations on the rising up of spectra in the eye
in its inflamed state, and their influence on ideas,' etc.[49]
Exactly what he means by *spectra* is made clear in a letter
to Godwin at the end of which he says: 'I bent down to
pick something from the ground, and when I raised my
head, I said to Miss Wordsworth, "I am sure, Rotha, that
I am going to be ill"; for as I bent my head there came a
distinct, vivid spectrum upon my eyes; it was one little
picture—a rock, with birches and ferns on it, a cottage
backed by it, and a small stream.'[50]*

When writing to Sir Humphry Davy, Coleridge describes
how as he lay in bed with inflamed eyes his 'voluntary ideas
were every minute passing, more or less transformed into
vivid spectra.'[52]* Wordsworth speaks of the imagination
as 'that intellectual lens through the medium of which
the poetical observer *sees* the objects of his observation,
modified both in form and colour. . . .'[359] During the
composition of *Werther*, a novel in the form of letters,
Goethe used first to imagine that some friend had called upon
him; then, walking to and fro before the chair on which
his guest was supposed to be sitting, Goethe conversed
with his imaginary visitor.[11] Turning to science: Clerk
Maxwell was in the habit of making a mental representation
of every problem.[34] Galton stated that on thinking for
example of a dog, the name disappeared but though he did
not actually visualize the appearance of a dog he found himself mentally in the same expectant attitude as he would be
if he were told a dog was coming round the corner; the sense
of an ill-defined spot that might shape itself into any

* See Lowes (John Livingston), *The Road to Xanadu*. London: Con
stable & Co., 1927, p. 66.

specified form of dog and that might jump, fawn, snarl, bark, or do anything else a dog might do but nothing else.[107]   This is the stage next to actual visualizing and sufficiently near to serve as an illustration.   Visualizing, however, is not confined to writers and scientists, for William Reed once asked Elgar how he produced the terrifying sound in *The Apostles* when Judas goes out and hangs himself.   Elgar replied that he just '*saw* Judas in the extremity of his remorse putting what he hoped to be an end to himself, and *heard* it on the muted horn.'[260]   It will be seen in Elgar's case as also in Daudet's that not only was the imagination worked up to the state of vision but also of audition.*

During the composition of a novel, of a poem, or when painting a picture, the imagination sometimes flows so rapidly that it is not practicable to pause and reason which course to take.   The hand must be so often behind the brain.   Conceptions if stared in the face by reason would fade and be gone.   Thus the thinker must at first, at any rate, trust to his feeling, instinct, intuition or whatever it may be called, to guide him, however much he may revise and check afterwards.   Learning to trust to feeling or instinct and knowing when and how far to trust it is an important part of the creative thinker's technique.   And the extent of the power of divination belonging to this faculty is shown by Lord Kelvin, who had at times to devise explanations of that which had come to him in a flash of intuition.[334]   Edison the inventor had also 'a weird ability to guess correctly'; this frequently enabled him to take 'short cuts to lines of investigation whose outcome has verified in a most remarkable degree statements apparently made offhand and without calculation.'[91]   Reiser states that Einstein when faced with a problem has a 'definite vision of its possible solution,'[261] in other words he *feels*, as we are accustomed to say, that the solution will be 'so and so' and he acts accordingly.   What is this feeling? Sir Joshua Reynolds describes it as 'the result of the accumulated experience of our whole life' and he cautions

* Mental Visions and Voices are of course well known to religious mysticism and those who care to pursue this subject further should consult Miss Evelyn Underhill's book *Mysticism*, twelfth edition. London: Methuen & Co., 1930, Part 2, Chapter V, 'Voices and Visions.'

his Academy Students against 'an unfounded distrust of the imagination and feeling, in favour of narrow, partial, confined, argumentative theories; . . . without considering those general impressions on the fancy in which real principles of *sound reason*, and of much more weight and importance, are involved, and, as it were, lie hid under the appearance of a sort of vulgar sentiment.' Reynolds says further that 'first thoughts, that is, the effect which anything produces on our minds, on its first appearance,' are never to be forgotten. These first thoughts if embodied in the picture will give it character; this is so because 'feeling' is the sum total of everything seen or heard by the artist and of everything that has passed through his mind; therefore, it must enrich the object towards which it is directed. It is necessary, therefore, to be on guard not to reconsider and correct these first thoughts.[264] Reynolds' advice can be applied not only to the arts but also in almost any other sphere.

Problems may arise in any subject and interrupt the flow of the work. The trouble may be due to a conflict between opposite tendencies and in this case a short rest may clear the mind. A mild stimulant will sometimes rectify matters. Lord Rayleigh would probably have said 'try a cup of tea'! for in his own case a difficulty would often be resolved after he had taken one.[256] Sheridan used to say 'if the thought is slow to come, a glass of good wine encourages it; and when it *does* come, a glass of good wine rewards it.'[242] In other cases the facts necessary to the solution of the problem may not at the time be available to the thinker. However, in ordinary cases a rest will often provide the cure. Sir John Millais, when baffled by some problem, would draw up a card-table in front of his picture, and, while he was dealing out the cards he used to glance now and then at his work. After a time, perhaps in an hour, he would suddenly jump up and with a few quick strokes with his brush, set everything right.[216] On one occasion when Sargent was entirely defeated by a string of opals he had to paint in a portrait, a rest during which he played a duet

by Fauré enabled him to paint the opals.[47] A night's rest
has often been found to bring the solution of a difficulty
in the morning. Swinburne sat down early one night to
write a poem with the refrain 'Only the song of a secret bird.'
To his astonishment the poem would not come. He retired
to bed in disgust. First thing upon waking on the following
morning he wrote the *Ballade of Dreamland* without a halt.[121]
Sir Walter Scott declared that the half hour between waking
and rising had always been 'propitious' to any composition
he had in hand. When he had any difficulty, a knotty
problem in a story, or a passage in a poem to fill in, it was
always when first he awoke in the morning that the desired
ideas came to him. 'This is so much the case,' Scott
declared, 'that I am in the habit of relying upon it, and
saying to myself when I am at a loss, "never mind, we shall
have it at seven o'clock to-morrow morning." '[281] Charlotte
Brontë told Mrs. Gaskell that it was not every day that she
could write. Sometimes weeks or even months elapsed
before she felt that she had anything to add to her story.
'Then, some morning she would waken up, and the progress
of her tale lay clear and bright before her, in distinct vision.'[110]
In cases when this plan of leaving the problem until the
morning is fruitless, there is nothing for it but to put away
the work and take up something else or go for a holiday.
Stevenson began to write *Treasure Island* at the rate of a
chapter a day until, at the beginning of the sixteenth
chapter he found he had lost hold. He was to spend the
winter at Davos and during the journey there he forced
himself to turn his mind to other matters. Arrived at
Davos he sat down one morning to find that the difficulty
had passed and that he was able to continue at the same rate
of composition as before.[300] Kipling, in his autobiography,
relates how in a difficulty he learnt to trust his personal
'Daemon.' When his story *The Eye of Allah* again and
again went dead under his hand and he could not tell why,
he put it away and waited. Then when he was meditating
upon something else his Daemon said 'Treat it as an
illuminated manuscript' and his problem was solved.[173]
There are various theories to account for this mysterious
phenomenon, the solution of a problem after a rest, and

when the mind is concentrated on some other matter, perhaps, but discussion of them must be left to the final chapter.

The main points in the general procedure after inspiration has taken place have now been described ; and briefly summarised they are as follows :—(i) The ideas occurring when in the glow of inspiration are (*a*) briefly noted down and (*b*) checked. (ii) (*a*) The subject is worked upon immediately, the thinker being wholly absorbed by it to the exclusion for the time being of everything else, or (*b*) The subject is set aside to develop and is then worked upon after an interval of time has elapsed, (*c*) the first draft of the completed work or half of it perhaps is put aside to 'mature' for a while ; then it is again revised before publication. (iii) Working at two or more subjects concurrently. (iv) Working up the imagination to the state of vision and sometimes of audition. (v) Trusting to feeling (or intuition, instinct). (vi) Procedure when baffled by a problem ; namely, laying the work aside and turning to something else. This process may be repeated many times during the course of a long work of any kind.

The point that must now be considered is what is to be done if inspiration itself does not come—if the ideas will not flow ? Isaac D'Israeli has drawn attention to a curious procedure of certain men of genius to awaken, or to use a colloquial expression, to 'start up' their inspiration by reading or playing over to themselves their favourite masters. He quotes as examples Gray, Malherbe, Corneille, Racine and Milton.[77] John Phillips, Milton's nephew, relates that his uncle spent the evenings 'reading some choice Poets, by way of refreshment after the days toyl, and to store his Fancy against Morning'[246] when he composed. It was noted as one of Sebastian Bach's peculiarities, that, though a master of improvisation, he never cared to begin with anything of his own but preferred first to play the work of some other master.[295]

There can be no doubt that many poets and writers wait for a definite 'call' before they begin to work. Montaigne, for example, said: 'I am no artist, but write as I feel the impulse.'[303]   Thomas Gray, in a letter to Dr. Wharton, declares that his resolutions about writing poetry were only made to be broken, and, 'after all,' he says, 'it will be just as the maggot bites.'[126]   In another letter to Wharton, Gray writes: 'I by no means pretend to inspiration, but yet I affirm that the faculty in question is by no means voluntary. it is the result (I suppose) of a certain disposition of mind, wch does not depend on oneself, & wch I have not felt this long time.'[127]   Woodhouse declared that Keats never sat down to write unless full of ideas and would leave off the moment he felt any dearth of them.[187]   On the other hand, Bailey declares that when Keats was writing the third book of *Endymion* in his rooms his daily task was fifty lines. Sometimes he fell short of this, but not often, and then he made it up on another day.[56]   George Crabbe was accustomed to write thirty lines of poetry on an average each day.[151]   Mrs. Browning says of her husband, 'Robert waits for an inclination, works by fits and starts; he can't do otherwise he says.'[236]   But later, W. M. Rossetti, speaking of Browning's method when composing the *Ring*, says that Browning wrote 'day by day on a regular systematic plan— some three hours in the early part of the day.'[273]   George Sand advised *M*. Charles Poncy to 'write only when possessed and urged by inspiration,' but herself worked regularly every night.   She showed *M*. E. M. Caro a plain table on which was a pile of large sheets of blue paper ready cut in quarto size.   'When you go this evening,' she told him, 'I shall set to work; and I shall not go to bed until I have filled twelve of these pages.'[39]   Léon Daudet says of his father that in youth he wrote only when 'fired by his subject,' but that in later life he worked regularly every day, and found that by so doing his brain became more supple in response to that discipline.[70]   Flaubert's prescription was 'Work patiently every day an equal number of hours, adopt the habit of a studious and calm life. . . .'[312]   'Constant work is the law of art as it is that of life,' said Balzac.[177]   Tchaikovsky's practice sums up that of all truly earnest and sincere thinkers.   Speaking of inspiration, he says, 'This guest does not always respond to the first invitation.   We must *always* work, and a self-respecting artist must not fold his hands on the pretext that he is not in the mood. If we wait for the mood, without endeavouring to meet it half-way we easily become indolent and apathetic. We must be patient, and believe that inspiration will come to those who can master their *disinclination*.'[317]

Getting into the right mood is often a matter of fighting disinclination but not entirely. It is essential that the environment be right. Balakirev found that in order to compose he needed absolute freedom and peace of mind.[33] There should also be freedom from interruptions. Dickens, speaking of interruptions, repeats the kind of thing that is so often said: 'It is only half-an-hour,—It is only an afternoon,—It is only an evening. . . .' 'they don't know,' he writes, 'that it is impossible to command one's self sometimes to any stipulated and set disposal of five minutes,—or that the mere consciousness of an engagement will sometimes worry a whole day.'[74] Interruptions are bad because they break the continuity of mood that is necessary for creative work of any kind. The question naturally arises whether solitude is or is not essential. To some undoubtedly it is; Lady Blessington records a conversation in which Byron said to her: 'Society and genius are incompatible, and the latter can rarely, if ever, be in close or frequent contact with the former, without degenerating : it is otherwise with wit and talent, which are excited and brought into play by the friction of society, which polishes and sharpens both. I judge from personal experience . . . if I have any genius. . . . I have always found it fade away, like snow before the sun, when I have been living much in the world. My ideas became dispersed and vague, I lost the power of concentrating my thoughts and became another kind of being. . . .'[21] Newton, Fontenelle declares, was 'passionately fond of his quiet.'[95] Henry Cavendish had a 'singular love for solitariness, and a reluctance to mix with his fellows.'[358] Darwin, in later life, saw few people outside his family. Turner, the landscape painter, liked to work in solitude.[139] Millais, in later life, allowed no one into his studio when he was painting because the slightest sound other than distant music broke the continuity of his thoughts. As he grew old he allowed one person at a time provided there was no moving about.[216] Balzac refused to see anyone when composing his novels.[176] Flaubert writes to Louis Bouilhet : 'I have just spent a good week, alone like a hermit, and as calm as a god. I abandoned myself to a frenzy of literature. . . .'[313] To balance these silence-loving men there are thinkers who like Priestley did not need solitude for their work. Priestley wrote by the parlour fire with his wife and children about him ; nor did their presence and occasional conversation disturb him.[337] Lord Kelvin's mathematical work was done 'when travelling by railway or at any time—but hardly ever alone' as conversation did not disturb him.[333] Turning to letters: Jane Austen had no study to retire to and must have done most of her work in the general sitting-room. Some authors not only do not need to be alone or in silence but work better for a certain amount of bustle going on around them. Thackeray once said: 'I cannot write comfortably in my own room. I do most of my compositions at hotels or at a club. There is an excitement in public places which sets my brain working.'[210] When Dickens began to write again after the rest of over two years he had taken since the close of *Martin Chuzzlewit*, he spoke of the difficulty of getting on quickly and supposed it was 'partly the effect of two years' ease, and partly of the absence of streets and numbers of figures.' 'I can't express how much I want these,' he says. 'It seems as if they supplied something to my brain. . . . For a week or a fortnight I can write prodigiously in a retired place (as at Broadstairs), and a day in London sets me up again and starts me. But the toil and labour of writing, day after day, without that magic lantern is IMMENSE!! . . .'[98] Mark Twain describes his working in Twichell's house with the noise of children and carpenters all around him. 'It's like a boiler factory for racket,' he declares, 'and in nailing a wooden ceiling on the room under me the hammering tickles my feet amazingly, sometimes, jars the table a good deal, but I never am conscious of the racket at all, and I move my feet into positions of relief without knowing when I do it.'[348]

A well-known modern writer, Edgar Wallace, on being

asked by Louise Morgan how ideas came to him, replied: 'They keep coming all the time. But I get most from sitting here by my window and watching people on the tops of buses, at midnight. I wonder about them, what kind of work they do for a living, what kind of houses they live in. . . .'[222B]

A musician might be supposed to object to noise and to be unable to work except in silence; but at least there are exceptions in Mozart and Schubert. General conversation did not disturb Mozart and he took part in it even when he was composing. Nor did music disturb him provided it did not interest him. Sometimes, at the Opera, Mozart would be engrossed with composing as his friends knew by the movements of his hands and the expression of his mouth as if whistling or singing.[156] Schubert wrote one of his most beautiful songs, *Ständchen*, sitting at a table in the gardens of 'Zum Biersack,' Währing, surrounded by a 'regular Sunday hubbub,' waiters running about, fiddlers and chatter. The song was written on the back of the bill-of-fare![143]

The kind of environment suitable for creative work is difficult to define. Some prefer silence while others enjoy bustle. Conversation disturbs some but not others. At all events the environment must be such that freedom and peace of mind are possible. Freedom from interruptions rather than solitude is the essential point not only because interruptions disturb or break the mood but because they are liable to cause shock. On one occasion when Chopin was playing to Madame Streicher his servant came in softly and placed a letter on the music-desk. With a cry Chopin stopped playing and his hair stood up on end. 'What I had hitherto regarded as impossible,' declared Madame Streicher, 'I now saw with my own eyes.'[235] As to noise, it has been shown that if it is more or less continuous some persons at least can tolerate it. The kind of noise to distract is a sharp sound : for example a dog barking. Schopenhauer relates how the cry of an animal would pierce between his thoughts and sever head from body as a headsman's axe.[364] A scratching pen or an unusual appearance in the lecture room of one of his students seriously disturbed a man so remarkable for concentration as Immanuel Kant.[304]

The times and seasons preferable for creative work must now be considered. On the whole it appears that morning or night hours are the most favourable to the flow of ideas. It has been shown that a difficulty unsolvable the day before is sometimes solved in the morning upon waking. In fact the value of morning hours when the mind is fresh has long been recognised as a time to be consecrated to important work. Arthur Schopenhauer, especially, set great store by morning hours and would not allow any interruptions at such times. Victor Hugo was up by six and began work after he had breakfasted.[290] Scott began about seven and worked except for the interval of breakfast, until one or two in the afternoon. Charles Reade worked as a rule from nine in the morning till three.[258] Milton was a very early riser. Toland says: 'In summer he would be stirring at four in the Morning, and in Winter at five. . . .'[338] Browning when writing the *Ring* worked for about three hours in the early part of the day.[273] Tennyson worked chiefly in the morning or in the evening.[322] Schubert, as a rule began to work early in the morning sitting upon his bed.[144] Beethoven rose at daybreak and went at once to his work-table and worked as a rule until two or three in the afternoon.[9] Tchaikovsky was seldom disinclined to work in the morning.[232] Coming to the present day and to a scientist: Pavlov said that the hour between eight-thirty and nine-thirty was the most favourable for creative work.[103]

Night-time when awake is one of the best times of all for the flow of ideas. It is not, however, practicable except to the very strong and then, usually only by fits and starts. Henri Poincaré tells how the solution to one of his problems came to him when lying in bed unable to sleep. Referring to this incident he says, 'I spoke of a night of excitement on which I worked as though in spite of myself. The cases of this are frequent. . . .'[251] It was during a sleepless night when racked by toothache that Pascal made his discovery concerning the Cycloid.[244] Edison the inventor did most of his inventing at night.[90] Balzac wrote mostly at night.[94] Schiller adopted the practice in order to be free from interruptions.[37] His neighbours heard him declaiming in the silence of the night. Byron also took advantage of night hours when writing *Don Juan*.[154]   Browning at one time used to spend the night-time wandering about a wood near Dulwich.   Many portions of *Paracelsus* and several scenes in *Strafford* originated in this way.[285]   D. G. Rossetti told Sir Hall Caine that his poem *Hand and Soul* except for 'an opening page or two' was composed 'all in one night in December, 1849, beginning about 2 a.m. and ending about 7. In such a case', he says, 'landscape and sky all unsurmised open gradually in the mind—a sort of spiritual Turner, among whose hills one ranges and in whose waters one strikes out at unknown liberty.   But I have found this only in night-long work, which I have seldom attempted, for it leaves one entirely broken. . . . '[208]   Several writers of more recent times have worked by choice at night. Madame Dostoevsky said her husband always worked at night.[80] Conrad, in early years, would sit far into the night.[59]   Mark Twain, when writing *The Innocents Abroad*, worked 'every night from eleven or twelve until broad day in the morning,' writing, as he says, 200,000 words in sixty days, the average was more than 3,000 words a day![348]   The spiritual alone-ness that comes over the thinker when the world sleeps, carrying with it that sense of detachment so essential to a creative thinker may account partly for the fascination and spell of working by night.   It is, however, a spell, to be resisted since it may lead to practices dangerous alike to bodily and mental health.   Byron, writing on Hollands and water,[105] Schiller on strong coffee, wine-chocolate, old Rhenish or Champagne,[38] the poet Crabbe at one time on weak brandy and water and snuff,[168] and Balzac on endless cups of strong coffee.[94]

Bodily posture is an important factor in the creative process.   The favourite attitude for thought would seem to be lying in bed and preferably in the morning.   Second to this is walking to and fro in a room or walking about in the country, a garden or the street.   And lastly composing while sitting on horseback or in a horse-carriage or a train. There can be no doubt that a little gentle exercise will often restore the mind when fatigued.   Beethoven used to go out into the open several times during the course of his long morning's work when he 'worked while walking.'[9] Mozart, in a letter already quoted, gives three positions favourable to his own creative mind : sitting travelling in a carriage, walking after a good meal, and at night when unable to sleep, presumably lying in bed.[211] Many of Tchaikovsky's themes were invented and his works planned during long solitary walks.'[233] Debussy as a very young man would often compose walking to and fro in a room.[182] Pasteur was accustomed, after he had dined, each night to pace the hall and corridor of his rooms at the Ecole Normale meditating the details of his work.[345] Adam Smith, when composing his books, usually walked up and down his room dictating to his secretary.[301] When ideas would not flow Victor Hugo used to walk about ; but his Pegasus he used to say was the knife-board of an omnibus.[290] Dickens, when composing *Little Dorrit*, complains to a friend that 'A necessity is upon me now—as at most times—of wandering about in my old wild way to think.'[74] When Scott was suffering from his seizures of cramp he used to dictate lying upon a sofa, but when a dialogue of special significance was in progress he would get up and walk up and down the room raising and lowering his voice as if acting the parts.[181] Burns often composed when 'holding the plough.' His guardsman remembered the poet turning up the mouse one day when ploughing.[240] Meredith held that a 'rapid walker poetically minded, gathers multitudes of images on his way.'[284] Of Mark Twain, his daughter says 'Some of the time when dictating, Father walked the floor . . . then it always seemed as if a new spirit had flown into the room.'[45] Schiller's neighbours often saw him walking rapidly to and fro and then throw himself into a chair and begin writing.[38] Albert Bielschowsky says that Goethe is speaking through the mouth of Wilhelm in *Die Wanderjahre* when that character reflects 'it often seems to me as though an invisible genius were whispering something rhythmical to me, so that on my walks I always keep step to it, and at the same time fancy I heard soft tones accompanying some song. . . .'[15]

Composing on horse-back has proved fruitful in the case of Goethe, Scott and Burns. Mozart's dislike of riding may have originated from the fear of being thrown when deeply engrossed in thought. Writing in a carriage was a frequent practice of Mozart's. Jahn quoting Rochlitz says that during his frequent carriage journeys, Mozart invented new melodies, arranged and elaborated them. The briefest notes preserved these studies and he used to keep scraps of music paper at hand when travelling, in the side-pocket of the carriage for such fragmentary notes and reminders; these scraps carefully preserved in a case, were a sort of journal of his travels to him.[157] Madame de Staël declared that she invented her plots in her palanquin.[297] Baron Cuvier used to read and write in his carriage and many of his most important memoirs were written as he drove through the streets of Paris.[178]

Lord Kelvin often worked at his mathematical studies when travelling by train.[333] Berlioz states that when composing the *Damnation de Faust* he wrote where he could, driving in a carriage, in railway-trains, or steam-boats, etc.[343] It is possible that the rhythmical movement of a carriage or train, of a horse and to a much lesser degree of walking, may produce on sensitive minds a slightly hypnotic effect conducive to that state of mind most favourable to the birth of ideas.

Lying in bed in the morning has ever been found to be favourable to the progress of thought. Richardson says that he had heard that Milton when dictating, usually, 'Sat leaning Backward Obliquely in an Easy Chair, with his Leg flung over the Elbow of it'; also, 'that he frequently Compos'd lying in Bed in a Morning,' and we learn from him, also, that Milton was unable to compose during the night.[268] Descartes lay in bed to a late hour. When perfectly awake he began to work, only half rising to note down his ideas.[134] Voltaire sometimes spent as many as sixteen to eighteen hours in bed, ringing for his secretary when there was any-thing to note down.[296] Coming to modern times, Clara Clemens says of Mark Twain·that 'lying in bed produced a more scintillating action of the mind.'[44] James Brindley, the great engineer, when faced with a difficulty would retire to bed and would remain there for one, two or three days until his problem was solved.[289] Thomas Moore, the poet, said 'It is singular the difference that bed makes, not only in the facility but the *fancy* of what I write . . . if I did not find that it relaxed me exceedingly, I should pass half my days in bed for the purpose of composition.'[218]   In the introductory lines to *Rhymes on the Road*, Moore makes humorous comment on the various positions of body adopted by authors and men of science when working[219]:

> 'WHAT various attitudes, and ways,
> And tricks, we authors, use in writing!
> While some write sitting, some like BAYES,
> Usually stand, while they're inditing.
> Poets there are, who wear the floor out,
> Measuring a line at every stride;
> While some, like HENRY STEPHENS,
> Pour out
> Rhymes by the dozen, while they ride.
> HERODOTUS wrote most in bed;
> And RICHERAND, a French physician,
> Declares the clock-work of the head
> Goes best in that reclin'd position.'

CHAPTER IV

SPECIAL PROCEDURE

INTRODUCTION : THE REALM OF THE IMAGINATION ITSELF
HAS ITS TRUTH

There is a passage in *M*. Ribot's well-known *Essay on the creative imagination*, in which he says :

'Esthetic imagination, when fully complete, is simply *fixed*, i.e., remains a fictitious matter recognised as such. It has a frankly subjective, personal character, arbitrary in its choice of means. A work of art—a poem, a novel, a drama, an opera, a picture, a statue, might have been otherwise than it is. It is possible to modify the general plan, to add or reduce an episode, to change an ending. The novelist who in the course of his work changes his characters; the dramatic author, who, in deference to public sentiment, substitutes a happy *dénoûment* in place of a catastrophe, furnish naïve testimony of this freedom of imagination. Moreover, artistic creation, expressing itself in words, sounds, lines, forms, colors, is cast in a mould that allows it only a feeble "material" reality.

The mechanical imagination is objective—it must be embodied, take on a form that gives it a place side by side with the products of nature. It is arbitrary neither in its choice nor in its means; it is not a free creature having an end in itself. In order to succeed it is subjected to rigorous physical conditions, to a determinism.'[267]

It will be seen from the quotation that Ribot says 'A work of art—a poem, a novel, a drama, an opera, a picture, a statue, might be otherwise than it is. It is possible to modify the general plan, to add or reduce an episode, to change an ending.' We know that a novelist does sometimes change an ending and that a painter will occasionally modify his picture at the suggestion of a patron, but the important thing is : how far can an artist alter his original conception if the work is to remain in any sense true? The works of the imagination being derived from the works of nature herself have no meaning unless they proceed and grow as nature herself

grows.   This means that they must be subject to a determinism.   This determinism is just as rigorous whether its object
is a work of art or a machine.   Moreover, there need not be
one way only in which the mechanic can group his pieces.
The variety in the escapements of clocks alone shows that
the mechanic has before him more than one way in which
he can group his pieces in order to produce an accurate time-
keeper.   The artist is bound to allow his idea to develop
naturally following where it leads him.   He knows that if he
obtrudes his own personal feelings he withers the natural
development of the idea and his honour as an artist is lost
because he has forsaken the truth.   A novelist will often
allow his characters to behave in a manner contrary to his
own personal inclination, because he knows it is in them to
behave so, and he will not force them into unlifelike actions.
There is a story of Thackeray when he was staying with Mr.
and Mrs. Bray, who were friends of George Eliot, that will
illustrate this point.   Thackeray was at that time composing the *Newcomes*.   When asked to allow Clive to marry
Ethel he replied that the characters once created *led* him,
and that he could not tell the events that waited on Clive and
Ethel.   On the following morning when Mrs. Bray asked
him if he had slept well he said, 'how could I, with Colonel
Newcome making a fool of himself as he has done?'   'But
why did you let him?' asked Mrs. Bray.   Thackeray : 'Oh, it
was in him to do it—he must.'[325]   On another occasion
Thackeray said 'I don't control my characters ; I am in their
hands, and they take me where they please.'[209]   When Balzac
was begged to save some wild young man or unhappy
woman among his creatures he would answer, 'Don't bother
me.   Truth above all.   These people have no backbone.
What happens to them is inevitable.'[175]   E. M. Caro says
that George Sand 'conceived her characters in a given
situation, which was nearly always a state of passion . . . she
would abandon herself to a kind of chance inspiration, which
produced the great struggles, controlling it so little . . . that
she did not know beforehand how these battles of life would
end, or how the novel would culminate.'[39A]   On the other
hand it is known that Dickens occasionally altered an ending
or modified a character.   But Mr. J. W. T. Ley states in a

note in his edition of *Forster's Life of Dickens* that as far as he knows there are very few instances of Dickens altering his purpose with a character.[99]   There is yet another case that should be mentioned since it shows to how great an extent a true artist is in the power of his characters and follows the natural development of his plot, however painful the result may be to him.   When the English publishers read *A Window in Thrums* they told Barrie that they thought it unbearably sad and warned him that the public does not like sad books. But Barrie would not alter the ending.   He says 'an author may not always interfere with his story, and if I had altered the end of *A Window in Thrums* I think I should never have had any more respect for myself.   It is a sadder book to me than it can ever be to anyone else.   I see Jess at her window looking for the son who never came back as no other can see her, and I knew that unless I brought him back in time the book would be a pain to me all my days, but the thing had to be done.'[137]   Daudet's advice to authors can be quoted at this point.   He says, 'you must enter into the person you are describing, *into his very skin*, and see the world through his eyes and feel it through his senses.   Direct intervention on the part of the writer is an error.'   On the other hand the theory of impassiveness is exaggerated.   He who tells a story has the right to be moved, himself ; but with discretion, and as it were behind the scenes, by the affairs of heroes and heroines, but without doing harm to that illusion which makes the charm.   All the live forces of the author are taken up by the expression of reality.'[72]   Joseph Conrad advised Galsworthy that 'In a book you should love the idea and be scrupulously faithful to your conception of life.   There lies the honour of the writer, not in the fidelity to his personages. . . . As against your people you must preserve an attitude of perfect indifference. . . .'[161]

   The true novelist, poet, musician, or artist is really a discoverer.   Ideas—the theme of a plot, a poem, a picture, a theme of music—come to him as a gift.   The idea, 'the seed-corn' as Brahms called it, he allows to develop naturally. There may come a point where it branches in one or many directions ; he is free at this point to follow one or other. And it is here and here only that the judgment or choice of the true artist may legitimately be exercised. In fact the artist is in much the same position as a gardener growing prize rose trees, who in order to produce beautiful roses lops off unwanted shoots and suckers. The artist may not alter the ending of his novel or the composition of his picture at *his* will because he has surrendered his will in order to follow out the nature of the conception. He may prune away irrelevances, he may, by choosing one or other of the possibilities before him, guide matters to some extent. But he is never free because the nature of the conception limits these possibilities: as Daudet said, 'the realm of imagination itself has its truth.'[72]

The artist and the man of science have, after all, not so different an outlook. Dr. June Downey, in her book *Creative Imagination*, notes the close relationship between the aesthetic and scientific attitudes, since both involve impersonality.[85] Gustave Flaubert, many years before, wrote to George Sand, 'that great art is scientific and impersonal.'[201]

The great artist in any medium is a discoverer and it may not be too far fetched to say that while the scientist creates a discovery the artist discovers a creation. The artist must follow the natural unfolding of his idea. Nature is his teacher whether he works in notes or colours, words or stone. As Sir Philip Sidney wrote in his *Apologie for Poetrie*, 'there is no Arte deliuered to mankinde, that hath not the workes of Nature for his principall object.'[287] But there is a class of art that is outside nature as we know her; for example the imp winking down from the cathedral pillar and the fairy stories that were the delight of our childhood. 'The Poet,' Sir Philip continues, 'disdayning to be tied to any such subiection, lifted vp with the vigor of his owne inuention, dooth growe in effect, another nature, in making things either better then Nature bringeth forth, or quite a newe formes such as neuer were in Nature, as the *Heroes*, *Demigods*, *Cyclops*, *Chimeras*, *Furies*, and such like: so as hee goeth hand in hand with Nature, not inclosed within the narrow warrant of her guifts, but freely ranging onely within the Zodiack of his owne wit.'[287] The true artist, faithful to the truths of the imagination 'goeth hand in hand with Nature' and is led by her to new discoveries and inventions.

THE NOVEL
'Without inspiration one can't of course begin anything,' Dostoevsky wrote to his brother.[81] Galsworthy remarks in one of his letters that 'Writers—not merely spinners of yarns to pocket pennies—require to be moved before they can write, some match must strike against the surface of their hearts or eyes. As a rule it is the unexpected, the peculiar, the—so to say—dramatic, that moves them; or it is something that violates their sense of proportion, or sets free emotions of love, of admiration, of anger, or of pity.'[199] Daudet used often to speak of the origin of *L'Arlésienne*. He heard two women calling to one another, one in a high shrill voice and the other in a deep one, across a plain at twilight; he felt they had impressed him in a singular way; then the plot of *L'Arlésienne* came to him 'as if in a sudden hallucination.'[73] Novelists search out for characteristic and moving subjects: Balzac went into the streets of Paris note-book in hand, a kind of literary Leonardo; Hardy made, as it were, thumb-nail sketches of the people that interested him and noted down aspects of nature, curious place-names and the like; Tolstoy listened to stories told him by his friends. Dumas encouraged people to bring him plots and themes to work up. Professor Maquet brought him the substance of that which eventually became *The Three Musketeers*.[188] But suitable material is not so easily discovered and, for this reason, dreams are sometimes found useful; their vivid mood or the strange and weird happenings they present with all the clarity of vision make them particularly fit to serve as the nucleus of a novel, poem or play. Sir Rider Haggard embodied one of his dreams in his story *The Mahatma and the Hare*.[133] Stevenson, in a 'Chapter on Dreams,' tells how his Brownies did half his work for him whilst he slept; and that he used some of these dreams in *The Strange Case of Dr. Jekyll and Mr. Hyde*, and again in his story *Olalla*.[299] Poe's favourite tale, *Ligeia*, Ingram states, was suggested by a dream.[155]

Mr. Walter de la Mare says of dreams: 'Like Mathematics, like Contemplation, like "Nonsense," Dream occupies a mental sphere of its own; and the debt owed to it by poetry, by all imaginative literature, is beyond computation.[73A]

Briefly, then, a theme suitable for an author to work up into a novel or a play must be distinguished by some striking characteristic, and must move him emotionally, otherwise his ideas will not flow. D. H. Lawrence said, 'I can only write what I feel pretty strongly about'.

From that which has already been said it would be supposed that the idea which is to be the germ of a novel or a play would be noted briefly and then after a suitable pause for revision work would begin in earnest ; or that the idea would be set aside to mature for a while. At all events it is important to realise that serious work does not usually begin at once. Dostoevsky said 'you evidently confuse the inspiration, that is, the first instantaneous vision, or emotion in the artist's soul (which is always present), with the *work*. I, for example, write every scene down at once, just as it first comes to me, and rejoice in it ; then I work at it for months and years.'[81] The fact is, that emotion can only be expressed retrospectively. Wordsworth, for example, in a passage which will be given later in full, says that poetry 'takes its origin from emotion recollected in tranquillity.'

The vivid impression has to sink back after briefly being noted so that it may be revived again purified from irrelevant details. The reason why it is advisable to allow a pause is because as Alexander Bain says 'the area of concentration is apt to be somewhat larger than the stimulating impression. . . . Hence our memory of some interesting scene or event often involves collaterals in close proximity with the exciting cause. The mind, being raised to a high pitch of intense consciousness, will seize hold of whatever crosses the view at the particular moment ; and matters irrelevant to the main stimulus will obtain a share of the resulting cohesive force of retention.'[5] Henry James, in the preface to his novel *The American*, said that in general he found it difficult to write of places under 'too immediate an impression—the impression that prevents standing off and allows neither space nor time for perspective. The image,' he continues, 'has had for the most part to be dim if the reflexion was to be, as is proper for a reflexion, both sharp and quiet. . . .'[160] There must, in fact, be a pause to allow the impression to settle down and to clear before work, as apart from first notes, should begin in real earnest.* If this pause is not allowed there will always be the danger of too much detail; or worse: a block may arise from irrelevant details obscuring the main issue. In cases where writers, George Sand, for example, appear to write at once without a pause; this is usually because the idea has been clearing, 'simmering' it is sometimes called, in their minds for some time beforehand.† George Sand would often sit silent *stupid* as she called it—whilst her admirers sang, played talked or argued around her[277]; and it was no doubt during these times that she both received new impressions and cleared others before setting to work on her nightly task.

Though the idea is first allowed to clear, it must not be thought from this that the actual working out takes place in cold blood. This is far from being the case. The vivid impression sinks back to be revived, cleared and refined and with the revived impression comes up also the emotion which accompanied it but in a subdued and controlled state, so that the judgment and all the powers of mind are active and in full play. The point is that the so-called fervour of composition is not the first inspirational fervour but a revival of it in a refined and controllable form. That there is and must be emotion when working out the idea is shown by the statements already quoted in which the authors experienced the feeling of compulsion and possession; and it is of course clear that the revived emotion will not be at the same intensity for every kind of subject and may also vary according to the author's temperament. The difficulty is to get the right intensity to ensure the flow of ideas and to maintain it. Tolstoy says he knows 'that when one is accustomed to work at a certain depth of creation, and cannot reach that depth, one cannot force oneself to it. (But then what joy it gives when one does attain it!) I am now in such a state. I have begun a mass of things, and all

---

* See Bullough (Edward), "Psychical Distance as a Factor in Art and an Aesthetic Principle". *Brit. Journal of Psychology*, Vol. 5, Pt. 2, June, 1912 (pp. 87-118).

† On reconsidering this sentence the author is unable to think of any writer other than George Sand who could finish a work and then start a new one without a pause. See p. 23.

things I love—only I cannot dive down to the proper depth, but keep floating up to the surface.'[194]

There are various means that are sometimes found helpful in preserving the right degree of intensity, such as working early in the morning or late at night, and also by working in a bright artificial light. Sheridan, when he wished to begin an important piece of work would rise at four in the morning and light up a great number of candles.[242] Scott, also, is said to have been fond of a profusion of lights. Elia prefers to eat, smoke, read and write by candle-light.[174] At other times the mood is revived or brought on by such simple means as the author's taking up and holding his pen in readiness to begin. The pen, in fact, seems to become a kind of fairy wand in the hands of some writers. According to Anne Ritchie, Thackeray 'used to say that from long habit he never could think so well as when he held his pen in his hand.'[326] It is good to picture Thackeray sitting gold pen in hand waiting for this necromancer's rod to compel the spell to work. Southey declared 'It is a very odd, but a marked characteristic of my mind,—the very nose in the face of my intellect,—that it is either utterly idle, or uselessly active, without its tools. I never enter into any regular train of thought unless the pen be in my hand; they then flow as fast as did the water from the rock in Horeb, but without that wand the source is dry!'[291] Madame de Staël found that when she took up her pen her brain seemed to become uncontrollable.[298] Galsworthy would sit pen in hand hoping that this expectant attitude would induce his thoughts to flow.[198] Many and strange indeed are some of the other devices that writers have used in the hope of getting themselves in the right frame of mind. Dumas, for instance, had to have coloured paper for his various types of literary work: blue for novels, pink for journalistic work, and yellow for poetry; nor would he write a novel with the same pen that he used for his plays.[189] Moore made humorous verse on this subject[219] :—

> 'Some bards there are who cannot scribble
> Without a glove, to tear or nibble;
> Or a small twig to whisk about—
> As if the hidden founts of Fancy,
> Like well of old, were thus found out
> By mystic tricks of rhabdomancy.

Such was the little feathery wand,
That held for ever in the hand
Of her,* who won and wore the crown
Of female genius in this age,
Seem'd the conductor, that drew down
Those words of lightening to her page.'

From what kind of nucleus is a novel evolved? This
question may be answered by Stevenson: he says there are
three ways and so far as he knows, 'three ways only, of
writing a story. You may take a plot and fit characters to
it, or you may take a character and choose incidents and
situations to develop it, or . . . you may take a certain
atmosphere and get action and persons to express and
realise it. I'll give you an example,' he said, '*The Merry Men*.
There I began with the feeling of one of those islands on the
west coast of Scotland, and I gradually developed the story to
express the sentiment with which that coast affected me.'[7]
The nucleus, then, may be a plot, one or more characters, or a
mood ; an emotional idea or an impression. How fragmentary this 'germ' may be is shown by a remark in a letter of
Mark Twain's to his mother : 'I am trying to think out a
short story. I've got the closing sentence of it all arranged
and it is good and strong, but I haven't got any of the rest
of the story yet.'[43] Here is another instance ; all that is
given by the inspiration is the closing sentence and a dim
notion of the plot : Daudet said that one evening, in front of
the Tuilleries, he had a vision of *Rois en Exil* and of the
sentence with which the book closes : 'A mighty thing lies
dead.'[73] It is difficult to point to any particular author and
say 'he began always with a plot ; she on the other hand,
with one or two characters ; he with an emotional idea.'
All three types of nucleus may occur at different times to the
same author as was the case with Stevenson.

It should be noted, however, that the greatest novels are
those in which the characters determine the plot, or such
plot as there may be, and have power of themselves to create
the atmosphere of farce, comedy or tragedy. By allowing
the characters to unfold themselves naturally the free
rhythm of life is preserved with all its changing moods and

* This refers to Madame de Staël.

shifting scenes.   When the plot is of paramount importance
or some philosophical idea dominates the author's mind, the
characters cannot have the same force or must occasionally
be made to act in a manner contrary to their nature.   Theo-
dore Dreiser has put the matter clearly for us: 'In all great
novels the plot is negligible.   In fact, where there is no plot
there is apt to be literary merit.   The reason for the absence
of plot in a great novel is that it interferes with the logical
working out of the destinies of the characters. The presence of
a plot obliges the novelist to make concessions here and there
so that the plot will work out to its proper *dénouement* . . . '[147A]

Melville states that Thackeray's 'plan was to create mentally two or three of the principal characters, and then to
write on from number to number, with only a general notion
of the course he would be taking a few chapters later.'[209]
Zola's method was to select the particular Rougon or Mac-
quart who was to be the chief character and then work outwards.   He knew the philosophical idea which was to govern
the work.   The next stage was to create secondary characters and such incidents and circumstances that might be supposed to belong to such characters.   Next, he worked at the
characters separately; their habits, appearance, history and
associations.   Then the environment of these characters had
to be studied.   Zola visited the localities where his novel
was supposed to be laid ; enquired into the professions of his
characters, visited places and people and studied technical
books.   The notes resulting from these enquiries were placed
in portfolios.   Zola then decided on the number of chapters
and distributed the material among them.   Before writing
he re-examined his material and re-arranged where necessary.[346]   Turning to a very different type of literature we
find Sir Rider Haggard working round a nucleus of which the
principal component is a dominant character.   He says that
in *She* 'that central idea was a woman who had acquired
practical immortality, but who found her passions remained
immortal too.   In *The Holy Flower*, . . . the central idea
is that of a gorilla which is worshipped as a god and periodic-
ally slays the king who holds his office as the brute's priest
and servant, with all the terrors that result from such a
situation.   In the case of both these books as of my others,

he declares, 'I had nothing more in my mind when I set myself to face them. Of course in such circumstances beginnings are hard—*c'est le premier pas qui coûte*—but after that the thing will generally evolve itself.[132]

Poe said 'I prefer commencing with the consideration of an *effect*. Keeping originality *always* in view. . . . Having chosen a novel first, and secondly a vivid effect, I consider whether it can be best wrought by incident or tone— whether by ordinary incidents and peculiar tone, or the converse, or by peculiarity both of incident and tone— afterwards looking about me (or rather within) for such combinations of event or tone as shall best aid me in the construction of the effect.'[248] For a story in which a special atmospheric effect is the principal feature it is essential for the author himself to get into the right mood—the corre-sponding mood. Sir Rider Haggard has pointed this out in the case of romance-writing. A romance, he says, should be written rapidly and not rewritten, 'since wine of this character loses its bouquet when poured from glass to glass.' The author when writing must 'live during its progress in an atmosphere quite alien to that of everyday life,' hence he must write with speed or his mood may be broken into by the concerns of this workaday world. The quality of his work will depend on this atmosphere being preserved during the period of composition.[132] The author must get into the mood, then the story will make itself. This is not so fantastic as it may seem, for by getting into the mood the ideas suitable to it will tend to be revived by the association of emotional states. The difficulty is to keep the mood when once it has been found. Dostoevsky says 'the tone and style of a story must make themselves. But true as that is, one occasionally loses one's note. . . . .'[82]

An author must be certain that his words express the particular shade of meaning that exactly embodies his idea. Flaubert writes to George Sand in defence of his own practice on this very point. He says : 'This anxiety for external beauty which you reproach me with is for me *a method*. When I discover a bad assonance or a repetition in one of my phrases, I am sure that I am floundering in error ; by dint of searching, I find the exact expression which was the only one and is, at the same time, the harmonious one. The word is never lacking when one possesses the idea.'[204] Mrs. Gaskell relates how precise and careful was Charlotte Brontë not only to be sure she knew exactly what it was she wished to say but that the words absolutely expressed her ideas. 'One set of words was the truthful mirror of her thoughts; no others, however apparently identical in meaning, would do. . . . She would wait patiently, searching for the right term, until it presented itself to her. It might be provincial, it might be derived from the Latin; so that it accurately represented her idea she did not mind whence it came; . . . . She never wrote down a sentence until she clearly understood what she wanted to say, had deliberately chosen the words, and arranged them in their right order.'[110]

But this is not all: the preparations for a great novel may be as elaborate as those for a work on history; for instance, Charles Reade made up his mind never to guess when it was possible to know.[257] Profound research may be necessary. The knowledge required to create a life-like character alone may be considerable. Jane Austen, for example, did not copy individuals; in common with all great artists she desired to create and not to reproduce.[4] The novel is not an imitative art; it is experimental. Given certain characters with such and such potentialities how would they react to a given situation? or conversely, given certain characters with certain potentialities what situation would result? The novelist sets himself to unravel these problems. Jane Austen allowed herself to note peculiarities and weaknesses but nothing more.[4] Mrs. Gaskell says that if Charlotte Brontë was 'struck by the force or peculiarity of the characters of some one she knew,' she analysed it to its germ, and 'took that germ as the nucleus of an imaginary character and worked outwards. . . .'[111] The character himself being settled there is his profession and environment to be studied. It will have been seen how much care Zola bestowed on this part of his preparatory studies. Hardy used to make notes in connection with some literary idea long before the work was actually begun.[149] So great sometimes is the work entailed before the author can begin to write that he experiences a kind of dread. Flaubert said 'on Saturday I begin *Bouvard et Pécuchet*! I tremble before it, as on the eve of embarking on a journey round the world.' And well he might. In connection with this work he read and annotated fifteen hundred books and was still engaged on writing this novel six years later when he died.[314] The method of work of another scholar and stylist, Walter Pater, may help to show that not by inspiration alone can a great novel be written. Pater's approach to a new task was at first in the spirit of careful analysis. In what way is Marius different from other men? he would say to himself. What is it that constitutes this difference: what is his 'Formula'? That is the type of question that Pater always asked himself before beginning a new work. And when he began to write he had by him, in addition to his notes, a piece of square blue paper with the 'Formula' or guiding thought of the work written upon it. He called these blue squares stars.

He began to write on small square slips of white paper and then to elaborate his ideas on larger squares. Finally he wrote out his work on full-sized sheets. The paper was ruled; and he left alternate lines blank for corrections. Even after this laborious work further polishing had to be done in proof. Like Voltaire, who thought the mind more enlightened when the eyes were satisfied, and like Balzac and Zola, Pater still needed the proof-sheets to inspire him to the fulfilment of his genius.[361]

There may arise in a novel through no fault of the author a situation or circumstance which from its very nature cannot be known to the author either from research or personal experience. What is to be done in such a case? An ordinary guess may be quite wrong. Charlotte Brontë, as it happens, worked out a technique to meet this difficulty. The knowledge of this comes to us from a question asked by Mrs. Gaskell concerning the description of the effects of opium in *Villette*. 'I asked her,' Mrs. Gaskell relates, 'whether she had ever taken opium, as the description given of its effects in "Villette" was so exactly like what I had experienced. . . . She replied, that she had never, to her knowledge, taken a grain of it in any shape, but that she had followed the process she always adopted when she had to describe anything which had not fallen within her own experience; she had thought intently on it for many and many a night before falling to sleep,—wondering what it was like, or how it would be,—till at length, sometimes after the progress of her story had been arrested at this one point for weeks, she wakened up in the morning with all clear before her, as if she had in reality gone through the experience, and then could describe it, word for word, as it had happened.'[113]

POETRY

'Poetry,' Shelley declares, 'is not like reasoning, a power to be exerted according to the determination of the will. A man cannot say "I will compose poetry." The greatest poet even cannot say it.'[286] Byron, when sailing on the ship *Hercules* was asked by his friends to compose verses on the Austrian tyranny in Italy. He tried and failed. Turning to his friends he said: 'You think it is as easy to write poetry as smoke a cigar,—look, it's only doggerel. Extemporizing verses is nonsense; poetry is a distinct faculty,—it won't come when called,—you may as well whistle for the wind. . . . I must chew the cud before I write. I have thought over most of my subjects for years before writing a line.'[341] To Moore, he said, in a letter, 'A man's poetry is a distinct faculty, or Soul, and has no more to do with the everyday individual than Inspiration with the Pythoness when removed from her tripod.'[222] In fact it seems to have been rather a case of hit or miss with Byron's poetry, for again he says, in a letter to Moore: 'I can never recast anything. I am like a tiger: if I miss the first spring, I go grumbling back to my jungle again; but if I *do hit* it is crushing.'[221]

The poet, like the novelist, will usually allow a pause between the inspiring impulse and the actual work. W. M. Rossetti says of Browning: 'he seldom or never, unless in quite brief poems, feels the inspiring impulse and sets the thing down into words at the same time—often stores-up a subject long before he writes it.'[273] In fact, Browning did not begin to write his great poem *The Ring and the Book* until four years after he had discovered and read the report of the Franceschini case.[237] Wordsworth's description of his own methods will serve to make clear this procedure. In the preface to the *Lyrical Ballads* he says: 'poetry is the spontaneous overflow of powerful feelings; it takes its origin from emotion recollected in tranquility; the emotion is contemplated till, by a species of reaction, the tranquility gradually disappears, and an emotion, kindred to that which was before the subject of contemplation, is gradually produced, and does itself actually exist in the mind. In this mood successful composition generally begins, and in a mood similar to this it is carried on. . . .'[360] Lady Blessington said of Byron, 'I observed that when, in our rides, we came to any fine point of view, Byron paused, and looked at it, as if to impress himself of the recollection of it. He rarely praised what had so evidently pleased him, and he became silent and abstracted for some time after. . . .' In explanation of this Byron remarked 'that as artists filled their sketch-books with studies from Nature, to be made use of on after-occasions, so he laid up a collection of images in his mind, as a store to draw on when he required them.' The reason why he remained silent was that 'he found the pictures much more vivid in recollection, when he had not exhausted his admiration in expressions, but concentrated his powers in fixing them in memory.'[22] Shelley's method of composing, fortunately preserved by Trelawny, shows how necessary it is to allow the inspiration to fade before work on the poem can begin in real earnest. It was Shelley's custom when in Italy, Trelawny relates, to wander off into the pine-forests near Pisa and there propped up against a fallen trunk he would allow the muse to take possession of him. On one occasion Trelawny found him thus propped up against a pine whose roots undermined by the water of a stagnant pool, had fallen across the water. The poet had been writing lines to a guitar and the manuscript in its several sheets lay beside him. 'I picked up a fragment,' Trelawny relates, 'but could only make out the first two lines:

"Ariel to Miranda: Take
This slave of music."

It was a frightful scrawl ; words smeared out with the finger, and one upon the other, over and over in tiers, and all run together . . . it might have been taken for a sketch of a marsh overgrown with bulrushes, and the blots for wild ducks ; such a dash-off daub as self-conceited artists mistake for a manifestation of genius. On my observing this to him, he answered : "When my brain gets heated with thought, it soon boils, and throws off images and words faster than I can skim them off. In the morning, when cooled down, out of the rude sketch, as you justly call it, I shall attempt a drawing." '[340] This vivid account shows how great is the flow of ideas during inspiration ; so many images speeding through his mind, that the poet has no time to think in case he loses something valuable. He hesitates, is almost certain, smears out and substitutes another word, when yet a further one appears : there is no time to choose ; all must go down ; half-a-dozen for the one word he will choose in the end. Words, yes, but not merely words to the poet : 'words that convey feelings, and words that flash images, and words of abstract notion, flow together, and whirl and rush onward like a stream, at once rapid and full of eddies.'[54] It will be seen, therefore, how necessary it is to allow a pause between the inspiration and the actual work on the poem.

A poem springs as a rule from some kind of 'germ.' Tennyson said more than once that his poems sprang often from a nucleus; a word or short phrase.[323] A story read or heard has often been a source of inspiration. Most of Whittier's ballads originated in this way.[171] Other poets find inspiration in the objects around them or their circumstances at the time when possessed by the poetic faculty. George Crabbe was always 'greatly stimulated by a snow-storm.' *Sir Eustace Grey* was written during a heavy fall of snow which confined him to the house.[169] Wordsworth said 'many of my poems have been influenced by my own circumstances when I was writing them. "The Warning" was composed on horseback, while I was riding from Moresby in a snow-storm. Hence the simile in that poem,

"While thoughts press on and feelings overflow,
And quick words round him fall like *flakes of snow.*"'

The 'Ecclesiastical Sonnets' furnish another example. The lines in No. XXI

'Within his cell,
Round the decaying trunk of human pride,
At morn, and eve and midnight's silent hour,
Do penitential cogitations cling:
Like ivy round some ancient elm they twine
In grisly folds and strictures serpentine;
Yet while they strangle, a fair growth they bring
For recompense—their own perennial power; —'

were suggested by a beautiful tree overgrown with ivy as described.[359]

Bielschowsky analyses certain of Goethe's compositions into aspects of his life at the time when composing them. The poem *Harzreise im Winter* he is able to analyse into the various stages of a journey that Goethe was taking when composing that poem. And we are to think, Bielschowsky says, of the poems *Willkommen und Abschied, Ilmenau, Wanderers Sturmlied* and *An Schwager Kronos* as having been thus evolved out of the circumstances of the poet's life.[13] Evidently Goethe and Wordsworth reacted as in a dream to their surroundings. Striking objects met with on a walk or ride became enwoven with the trend of their thoughts as symbolic illustrations of them. Sometimes, when on a solitary walk, a line of verse, or a stanza or so apparently having nothing to do with his present surroundings will come into the poet's mind. Concerning the origin of the *Hunting of the Snark* Lewis Carroll writes: 'I was walking on a hill-side, alone, one bright summer day, when suddenly there came into my head one line of verse—one solitary line—"For the Snark *was* a Boojum, you see." I knew not what it meant, then: I know not what it means, now: but I wrote it down: and, some time afterwards, the rest of the stanza occurred to me, that being its last line: and so by degrees, at odd moments during the next year or two, the rest of the poem pieced itself together, that being its last stanza[40A]. A modern poet, Housman, describes this experience and how he treated it thus : 'Having drunk a pint of beer at luncheon—beer is a sedative to the brain, and my afternoons are the least intellectual portion of my life—I would go out for a walk of two or three hours. As I went along, thinking of nothing in particular, only looking at things around me and following the progress of the seasons, there would flow into my mind, with sudden and unaccountable emotion, sometimes a line or two of verse, sometimes a whole stanza at once, accompanied, not preceded, by a vague notion of the poem which they were destined to form part of. Then there would usually be a lull of an hour or so, then perhaps the spring would bubble up again. . . . When I got home I wrote them down, leaving gaps, and hoping that further inspiration might be forthcoming another day. Sometimes it was, if I took my walks in a receptive and expectant frame of mind ; but sometimes the poem had to be taken in hand and completed by the brain, which was apt to be a matter of trouble and anxiety, involving trial and disappointment and sometimes ending in failure.'[150]

Another source of inspiration is purely emotional. The death of a friend, for example, inspired *Lycidas* and *In Memoriam* and excited most of Gray's important poems.[120] Music is another type of purely emotional stimulus. Moore's *Irish Melodies* and 'Scots, wha hae wi' Wallace bled,' the famous Bannockburn ballad which Burns composed to an old Scotch tune 'Hey tutti taitie' that had often brought tears to his eyes when played on 'Frazer's Hautboy,' are instances of poetic inspiration coming in response to a theme of music. Burns says of this old tune that he had heard 'in many places of Scotland, that it was Robert Bruce's March at the battle of Bannock-burn.—This thought,' he says, 'in my yesternight's evening walk, warmed me to a pitch of enthusiasm on the theme of Liberty & Independence, which I threw into a kind of Scots Ode, fitted to the Air, that one might suppose to be the gallant ROYAL SCOT's address to his heroic followers on that eventful morning.'[30]

This emotional stimulus leads on to consideration of the

poetic mood. Strictly speaking, every kind of nucleus sets the poet or novelist into its own mood. As Yeats declares : 'Literature differs from explanatory and scientific writing in being wrought about a mood or continuity of moods...'[363A] Schiller, in a letter to Goethe referring to his poem *The Casting of the Bell* says : 'This poem I have much at heart, but it will take me several weeks, as I require to get myself into so many different kinds of dispositions. . . .'[279] The poet as well as the novelist has to get himself into the mood of his piece and then the poem will evolve of itself. For example, Goethe wrote to Eckermann : 'the measure comes as thought unconsciously from the poetic mood.'[15] Bielschowsky states that it sometimes happened with Goethe that the rhythm came into existence before the text.[15] This is of great significance because it shows that at least in some types of poetical genius there is an analogy between poetic and musical inspiration. The measure coming first calls to mind at once Goethe's great contemporary, Beethoven, the second movement of whose string quartet *opus* 59, No. 1, begins with a rhythmical subject.* In a passage already quoted it was seen how Goethe put into the mouth of Wilhelm in *Die Wanderjahre* what was probably his own experience : 'It often seems to me as though an invisible genius were whispering something rhythmical to me, so that on my walks I always keep step to it, and at the same time fancy I hear soft tones accompanying some song, which then comes to me in one way or another and delights me.'[15] Schiller writes to Goethe : 'The preparations for so complicated a work as a drama set the mind in a strange state of motion. Even the very first operation of seeking a certain method in the work—so as not to grope about aimlessly—is no trifling affair. I am at present engaged with the skeleton, and find that in a dramatic structure, as in the case of the human body, it is the most essential part. I should like to know how you set to work in such matters. With me the conception has at first no definite or clear object ; this comes later. A certain musical state of mind precedes it, and this, in me, is only then followed by

* The *Allegretto vivace e sempre scherzando.*

the poetic idea.'[278]   This musical state of mind calls to remembrance the declaration of Sydney Dobell that anyone who would wholly understand his poetry 'lyrical or otherwise —must read it with the mind of a musician. I don't mean,' he says, 'that it is *musical*, in the common sense, but that it is written on the principles of music, *i.e.* as a series of combinations that shall produce certain *states* in the hearer, and not a succession of words which he is separately to "intellectualate" by the dictionary.'[164]*

We have seen that Burns found inspiration in a musical theme for his famous ballad *Bannockburn*. Many of Burns's lyrics originated in this way; the poet drawing his inspiration from an old folk-tune. 'My way,' says Burns, 'is: I consider the poetic Sentiment correspondent to my idea of the musical expression; then chuse my theme; begin one Stanza; when that is composed, which is generally the most difficult part of the business, I walk out, sit down now & then, look out for objects in Nature around me that are in unison or harmony with the cogitations of my fancy & working of my bosom; humming every now & then the air with the verses I have framed: when I feel my Muse beginning to jade, I retire to the solitary fireside of my study, and there commit my effusions to paper; swinging at intervals on the hind-legs of my elbow-chair; by way of calling forth my own critical strictures, as my pen goes on.—Seriously this, at home, is almost invariably my way.'[31] This procedure, summed up is simply that the poet is moved by the folk-tune. The mood of the tune suggests a poetical theme of similar mood. The poet composes a stanza, then goes out and deliberately collects

---

* Concerning the influence of music on the composition of drama Mr. Bernard Shaw made a very interesting statement at the Malvern Festival in 1939. He said 'My method, my system, my tradition, is founded upon music. It is not founded upon literature at all. I was brought up on music when I was young.

. . . . . .

'I did not read plays very much because I could not get hold of them, except, of course, Shakespeare, who was mother's milk to me. What I was really interested in was musical development.

'If you study operas and symphonies you will find a useful clue to my particular type of writing. If you want to produce anything in the way of great poetic drama you have to take a theme, as Beethoven did in his symphonies, and keep hammering at the one theme. . . .' (*Sheffield Daily Telegraph*, 15 August, 1939.)

additional material in accordance with the mood, sad, gay, mournful or whatever it may be. He keeps the mood going by humming his verses, as he makes them to the tune. Deliberately collecting material in this way may seem a rather cold-blooded and matter-of-fact way of composing a poem, but it does not appear to be unusual. For example, Whitman told H. S. Morris, who fortunately noted down his words, that 'an idea would strike him, which after mature thought, he would consider fit to be the "special theme" of a "piece".' This he would revolve in his mind in all its phases, and finally adopt, setting it down crudely on a bit of paper,—the back of an envelope or any scrap,—which he would place in an envelope. Then he would lie in wait for any other material which might bear upon or lean toward that idea, and, as it came into his mind, he would put it on paper and place it in the same envelope. After he had quite exhausted the supply of suggestions, or had a sufficient number to interpret the idea withal, he would interweave them in a "piece" as he called it. 'I asked him,' Morris says, 'about the arrangement or succession of the slips, and he said "they always fall properly into place."'[172] Poe's manner of composing was at times even more matter of fact than Whitman's; he even disclaims inspiration itself! Fortunately he has left a careful analysis of his procedure when composing *The Raven*. This analysis is nearly eleven pages; and it is, therefore, far too long to quote in full. Poe begins by saying that no one point in its composition is referable either to accident or intuition—that the work proceeded step by step to its completion with the precision and rigid consequence of a mathematical problem. The length, he decided, should be one hundred lines; actually in the end it was one hundred and eight. The poem was to be *universally* appreciable. Beauty being the sole aim of a poem this poem must be beautiful. By beauty men think not of a quality as supposed, but of an effect—'an intense and pure elevation of soul.' What was the *tone* of beauty's highest manifestation—*sadness*. Therefore the tone of the poem must be melancholy. Next he sought for some 'artistic piquancy' which might serve as the keynote in the construction of this poem. The refrain was frequently used, thereby proving its value; a refrain therefore, should be the key-note. As a corollary the poem would be divided into stanzas each ending with the refrain. The refrain depends for its effect on the force of monotone; this led to the choice of a single word. The question now arose as to the character of that word. The single-word refrain to be effective must be 'sonorous and susceptible of protracted emphasis,' this led to the long O as the most sonorous vowel in connection with R as the most producible consonant. Poe searched for a word melancholy in character embodying these two letters, O and R. The word 'nevermore' occurred to him at once as fulfilling the conditions. A pretext had to be found for the continuous use of the word 'Nevermore' by a human being. The difficulty arose in combining monotony with the exercise of reason : this led to the idea of allowing the word to be repeated not by a reasoning being such as a human but by a non-reasoning being capable of speech. Naturally a parrot suggested itself; but this idea was given up in favour of the Raven as equally capable of speech and more in keeping with the melancholy tone. He had now the conception of a Raven, the bird of ill-omen, monotonously repeating the word 'Nevermore' in a poem of melancholy tone of the length of one hundred lines. Poe then asked himself, what is the most melancholy topic according to the *universal* under-standing of mankind? Death was the obvious answer. And when was death most poetical? —when it closely allied itself to *Beauty* : the death of a beautiful woman. The lips most suited to this topic are those of a bereaved lover. Poe had now to combine the ideas of a lover lament-ing his deceased mistress with a Raven monotonously repeating the refrain 'Nevermore.'[249]

This summary of a part only of Poe's analysis will be enough to show with what extreme care and reasoning a poem may have to be constructed. This careful procedure is not unknown in other famous poets. Oliver Goldsmith, Forster relates, when composing *The Deserted Village*, used first to sketch a part of his design in prose, throwing out ideas as they occurred to him; next he sat down to versify them, correct and add other ideas better suited to the subject.

Sometimes he exceeded his prose design by writing several verses impromptu. These verses he revised with great care lest they should be found unconnected with his main design.[96] W. M. Rossetti states that Robert Browning's method of composing was 'to write down on a slate, in prose, what he wants to say, and then turn it into verse, striving after the greatest amount of condensation possible: thus if an exclamation will suggest his meaning, he substitutes this for a whole sentence.'[272] But while this must not be thought to be Browning's *invariable* method it is possible that the practice of first writing out in prose the substance that he wishes to express in verse has been resorted to by many distinguished poets. The Poetical Works of S. T. Coleridge, edited by Ernest Hartley Coleridge, contain prose versions of two poems: 'Glycine's Song' from *Zapolya* and 'Why is my Love like the Sun?'[54A]

When Louise Morgan asked Yeats what gave rise to the initial impulse of a poem he told her 'Some situation in life— a sudden emotion. My poems all originate like that. The idea for a poem comes in moments of personal excitement. I sometimes jot down a few *prose lines* in a note book, leaving them purposely vague. Then begins the process of gradually giving the poem rhymical form.'[222A]

From the examples given of methods of work of certain well-known poets it is clear that there are two main types of inspiration which will give rise to a poem; that which provides content and versification together as a gift of the automatic activity of the poet's brain; and that which provides content or some content, coupled with a powerful mood or emotional stimulus, or a mood alone. With this second type of inspiration further material is collected in accordance with the mood as we saw by the methods of work of Whitman and of Burns; and when all is ready versification is then deliberately taken in hand.

Edgar Allan Poe would have us believe that no part of *The Raven* owed its existence to inspiration but that all was logically thought out. Few poems, however, arise entirely from either type of inspiration. Goldsmith's deliberate versification of *The Deserted Village* was sometimes interrupted by a few lines presented to his mind as a gift. And Housman, whose poems were clearly automatic in character, confesses that the fount would sometimes run dry in the middle of a poem and he would then have to compose the missing section of his own will.

The inspiration which gives rise to a poem must be checked no less than inspiration in any other subject. How is a poem to be checked? 'Shall I give you an infallible little rule for verse?' writes Voltaire to Helvétius, 'Here it is. When a thought is just and noble, something still remains to be done with it: see if the way you have expressed it in verse would be effective in prose: and if your verse, without the swing of the rhyme, seems to you to have a word too many—if there is the least defect in the construction—if a conjunction is forgotten—if, in brief, the right word is not used, or not used in the right place, you must then conclude that the jewel of your thought is not well set. Be quite sure that lines which have any one of these faults will never be learnt by heart, and never re-read: and the only good verses are those which one re-reads and remembers, in spite of oneself.'[311]

What are the times and seasons most favourable to poetic inspiration? If one season more than another is propitious then that season is autumn.

> '... there is a harmony
> In Autumn, and a lustre in its sky,
> Which thro' the summer is not heard or seen,'

Aubrey, quoting Phillips, says of Milton: 'All the time of writing his *Paradise Lost*, his veine began at the Autumnall Æquinoctiall and ceased at the Vernall or thereabouts (I believe about May) and this was 4 or 5 yeares of his doeing it.'[2] George Crabbe thought 'Autumn the most favourable season of the year for poetical composition.'[169] Burns used to say 'Autumn is my propitious season, and I make more verses in it than in all the year else.'[240] As to the time of day: some poets prefer night-time and the inspiration of the candle—Alfred de Musset, when the muse possessed him, used to collect all the candlesticks in the house.[225] 'Night and silence call out the starry fancies' declares Elia and he asserts that 'No true poem ever owed its birth to the sun's light.'[174] Other poets prefer the morning: John Phillips says of Milton 'hee waking early (as is the use of temperate men) had commonly a good Stock of Verses ready against his Amanuensis came; which if it happened to bee later than ordinary, hee would complain, Saying *hee wanted to be milkd.*'[246] The open air seems to be one of the conditions of inspiration for many poets. Shelley told Trelawny that 'In composing, one's faculties must not be divided; in a house there is no solitude : a door shutting, a footstep heard, a bell ringing, a voice, causes an echo in your brain and dissolves your visions.' 'He told me,' Trelawny says, 'that he always wrote best in the open air, in a boat, under a tree, or on the bank of a river. There was an undivided spirit,' he said, 'which reigns abroad, a sympathising harmony amongst the works of Nature, that made him better acquainted with himself and them.'[339] Coleridge said 'I never find myself alone, within the embracement of rocks and hills, a traveller up an alpine road, but my spirit careers, drives and eddies, like a leaf in autumn ; a wild activity of thoughts, imaginations, feelings, and impulses of motion rises up from within me. . . .'[61]

For certain poets, twilight is the most favourable time for poetic inspiration. Burns, for example, found that at twilight his mind was most active[241] and the poet Thomas Moore also : in semi-humorous verse he says :

> 'That bards, who deal in small retail,
> At home may, at their counters, stop;
> But that the grove, the hill, the vale,
> Are Poesy's true wholesale shop.
> And, verily, I think they're right—
> For, many a time, on summer eves,
> Just at that closing hour of light,
> When like an Eastern Prince, who leaves
> For distant war his Haram bow'rs,
> The Sun bids farewell to the flow'rs,
> Whose heads are sunk, whose tears are flowing
> Mid all the glory of his going!—
> Ev'n *I* have felt, beneath those beams,
> When wand'ring through the fields alone,
> Thoughts, fancies, intellectual gleams,
> Which, far too bright to be my own,
> Seem'd lent me by the sunny Pow'r,
> That was abroad at that still hour.'[219]

A man cannot compose poetry unless he possesses the poetic faculty. What is this faculty? What in short are the qualities that a man must cultivate in order to be a poet? 'First we require in our Poet,' says Ben Jonson, '. . . a goodness of natural wit. For whereas all other arts consist of doctrine and precepts, the poet must be able by nature and instinct to pour out the treasure of his mind.'[165]   Secondly he must have that particular quality which goes 'to form a Man of Achievement especially in Literature, and which Shakespeare possessed so enormously—I mean,' said Keats, '*Negative Capability*, that is, when a man is capable of being in uncertainties, mysteries, doubts, without any irritable reaching after fact and reason—Coleridge, for instance, would let go by a fine isolated verisimilitude caught from the Penetralium of mystery, from being incapable of remaining content with half-knowledge.'[166]   The reason why 'Negative Capability' is so essential is explained by a passage in which W. B. Yeats says: 'The more a poet rids his verses of heterogeneous knowledge and irrelevant analysis, and purifies his mind with elaborate art, the more does the little ritual of his verse resemble the great ritual of Nature, and become mysterious and inscrutable.   He becomes, as all the great mystics have believed, a vessel of the creative power of God. . . .'[363]   'I soon found,' said Socrates, 'that it is not by wisdom that the poets create their works, but by a certain natural power and by inspiration, like soothsayers and prophets, who say many fine things, but who understand nothing of what they say.'[247]

> 'Since in their thoughts, as in a glass,
> Shadows of heavenly things appear,
> Reflections of bright shapes that pass
> Through other worlds, above our sphere!'[219]

The poet must be content to reflect the impressions that come to him expressing them by means of 'elaborate art.' He should not attempt to analyse these shadows since knowledge is selection and by selecting much is lost by the way: the presentation becomes less scenic and natural. Goethe even, with all his skill, felt that words were 'foppish' and would have preferred to 'speak like Nature, altogether in drawings.'[14]

It is the business of the poet, Yeats declares, to make the 'little ritual of his verse resemble the great ritual of Nature.' In order to do this he must possess the poetical character. What, is the poetical character like? Keats replies: 'it has no self—it is everything and nothing— It has no character—it enjoys light and shade; it lives in gusto, be it foul or fair, high or low, rich or poor, mean or elevated—It has as much delight in conceiving an Iago as an Imogen. What shocks the virtuous philosopher, delights the camelion Poet.' Then Keats goes on to explain that a poet has 'no Identity.'[167] The poet is a passive being so far as his poetry is concerned; he becomes as it were for the time-being one with the objects that interest him; since he is 'continually in for—and filling some other Body. . . .' 'When I am in a room,' Keats continues, 'with People, if I ever am free from speculating on creatures of my own brain, then not myself goes home to myself: but the identity of every one in the room begins to press upon me that I am in a very little time an(ni)hilated—not only among Men; it would be the same in a Nursery of children. . . .' And he says that no one word he utters can be taken for granted as an opinion growing out of his identical nature.[167] This impersonal attitude—the poetical character—is in fact a kind of submission to the laws of the imagination and to its truth. The poet, for the time being, surrenders himself and his views and wishes completely to enter into the subject he is writing about.

The poet then must have a goodness of natural wit, negative capability and the poetical character. 'To this perfection of nature in our Poet,' says Ben Jonson, 'we require exercise of those parts, and frequent. . . . If his wit will not arrive suddenly at the dignity of the ancients, let him not yet fall out with it, quarrel, or be over-hastily angry; offer to turn it away from study in a humour, but come to it again upon better cogitation; try another time, with labour. If then it succeed not, cast not away the quills yet, nor scratch the wainescot, beat not the poor desk, but bring all to the forge, and file again; turn it anew.'[165] But we will add turn if not too many times, for, as Keats said, 'That if poetry comes not as naturally as the leaves to a tree, it had better not come at all.'[187]

CHAPTER V

SPECIAL PROCEDURE [Continued]

MUSIC

Music and poetry may be said to represent the two opposite sides of the same medal. The poet, by means of words and rhythm calls up visions before the mind's eye. In many cases the actual dictionary meaning of the words seems often to be no more than a rough explanatory guide to the mental images the words evoke. The musician, by the use of notes and rhythm, is also able to call up emotions and visions; but in a greater range owing to his more subtle medium, than the poet. Tchaikovsky speaks of music as being 'a purely lyrical process. A kind of musical shriving of the soul, in which there is an encrustation of material which flows forth again in notes, just as the lyrical poet pours himself out in verse. The difference consists,' he says, 'in the fact that music possesses far richer means of expression, and is a more subtle medium in which to translate the thousand shifting moments in the mood of a soul.'[316] Poetry has the advantage for some of conveying a more definite meaning; but music is really the most poetical, since in its very elusiveness to positive interpretation it is mysterious and inscrutable as nature herself. Who standing and gazing at a landscape could divine its meaning? And yet the landscape is full of meaning with significance so great that it is beyond interpretation.

Music like poetry is built up around a mood or series of moods, but the musical mood requires for its embodiment no concrete idea as does poetry. Tchaikovsky makes this point clear in a letter to the Grand Duke Constantine Constanti-novich. He says that 'for a lyrical poem, not only the mood, but the idea, must be there . . . In music it is only necessary to evoke a certain general mood or emotion. For example,' he continues, 'to compose an elegy I must tune myself to a melancholy key. But in a poet this melancholy must take some concrete expression. . . .'[321] Elsewhere he refers to the changing mood to which no concrete meaning can be attached. 'You ask if in composing this symphony I had a special programme in view. To such questions regarding my symphonic works I generally answer: nothing of the kind. In reality it is very difficult to answer this question. How interpret those vague feelings which pass through one during the composition of an instrumental work, without reference to any definite subject?'[316]

Debussy, on the other hand, compares music with painting. He says, 'Gather impressions. But don't hurry to note them down; for music has this over painting, that it can bring together all manner of variations of colour and light. It is a point that is not often observed though it is quite obvious.'[186]

Music is, then, a highly sensitive medium, capable of reflecting with the accuracy of a mirror those fleeting sensations and changing moods that sweep the mind of the artist like clouds in a summer sky. The procedure for music is in general much the same as that for poetry and novel-writing. We have seen how Sir Rider Haggard insists on the special mood and its preservation as being essential to romance-writing. Debussy said 'one can never spend too much time constructing that special atmosphere in which a work of art should move. I believe that one should never hurry to write but leave everything to that many-sided play of thoughts—those mysterious workings of the mind which we too often disturb. . . .'[185] In order to preserve the mood and to allow those 'mysterious workings of the mind' it is usually necessary, as Tchaikovsky says, for a 'composer to shake off all the cares of daily existence, at least for a time, and give himself up entirely to his art life.'[318] Wagner, speaking of his own genius, declares that it consists in the 'unitive power which binds and fuses ordinary talents so that their combined strength when exerted achieves things technically impossible by an individual talent. This unitive principle is, I believe, complete absorption—forgetfulness of self and of the world about me, a capacity to saturate all my being unreservedly with my subject, which—protected thus from trivial contacts—grows in depth and intensity.'[350] For the working out of ideas he found that complete quiet was necessary. 'I know that the only way to achieve my end,' he says, 'is to let my mind rove back again into the realm of dreams.'[351]   The principle is the same in all lines of artistic creative thought : the ideas must be allowed to flow, combine and branch naturally so that the finished production, be it poem, novel, opera or symphony, comes into being and develops like a natural object.   In order to bring this to pass the environment must be right.   Wagner's study, Mr. Newman tells us, had soft carpets and curtains giving a subdued light.   There were no objects with sharp lines to disturb or distract his contemplation; even books were removed and a sweet perfume scented the room.[230]   On the other hand, there have been several of the first rank who did not require complete quiet for the working out of their ideas.   We have already noted in this category, Mozart, Schubert and Berlioz.   Sir Hubert Parry's name can now be added to this list.   His power of concentration was so intense that he could compose on a corner of the dining-room table whilst a meal was being laid or cleared away.[124]   But these composers are none the less occupied with musical thoughts. Mozart seemed always to be absorbed with his own thoughts even when conversing.   Tchaikovsky says: 'sometimes I observe with curiosity that uninterrupted activity, which—independent of the subject of any conversation I may be carrying on—continues its course in that department of my brain which is devoted to music.   Sometimes it takes a preparatory form—that is, the consideration of all details that concern the elaboration of some projected work ; another time it may be an entirely new and independent musical idea, and I make an effort to hold it fast in my memory. . . .'[318]

Emotion can, as a rule, only be expressed retrospectively as in the arts of poetry and novel-writing.   Tchaikovsky says, 'those who imagine that a creative artist can—through the medium of his art—express his feelings at the moment when he is *moved*, make the greatest mistake. Emotions—sad or joyful—can only be expressed *retrospectively*, so to speak.'[318]   A period must be allowed for the emotion to sink back and clear before work in real earnest can begin.   Brahms emphasizes this point.   After speaking of the musical inspirational 'germ' as a gift which he can not further or encourage, he says, 'At the time I must disregard this "gift" as completely as possible but ultimately I have to make it my own inalienable property by incessant labour. And that will not be quickly accomplished. The idea is like the seed-corn; it grows imperceptibly in secret. When I have invented or discovered the beginning of a song . . . I shut up the book and go for a walk or take up something else; I think no more of it for perhaps half a year. Nothing is lost, though. When I come back to it again it has unconsciously taken a new shape, and is ready for me to begin working at it.'[104] Wagner once left off composing for nearly six years in order to clear his mind and bring, as he says, 'its darkling things to the clear light of consciousness.'[349] Debussy said: 'I sometimes require weeks to decide on one harmonious chord in preference to another.'[184] On the other hand, occasionally a piece of music will come complete, or almost so, just as occasionally a poem comes out in its entirety. Schubert's songs often appear to have come straight away. When he had read the Erlkönig several times over in quick succession he wrote it down so rapidly 'that the very notes seemed to tumble over one another.'[145] Once when Schubert was asked to set a poem by Grillparzer entitled *Zögernd leise in des Dunkels nächt'ger Stille*, he merely took the verses to the window; read through the poem twice with deep attention; then, turning round, he said with a smile, 'I have it, it's done already, and it will do very well.'[145] For long works, however, inspiration usually gives only the skeleton and general hints as to how it is to be filled in. The writing and re-writing of almost every bar of Beethoven's works will give an idea of the extreme labour involved; though perhaps Beethoven is an extreme case. Here for example is Weber composing an opera given in the words of his son, Max von Weber: 'Many a time, in the autumn, might he be seen on the Brühlische Terrasse, or in the Grosser Garten, at hours when the fashionable world of Dresden was not there, with some closely-written pages in his hand, which he stood still and read, and then wandered on muttering to himself. He was learning by heart the words of "Euryanthe." He studied them until he made them a portion of himself—his own creation as it were . . . the genius of the composer would sometimes lie dormant during his frequent repetition of the words ; and then suddenly the idea of a whole musical piece would flash into his mind like a sudden gleam of light into the darkness. It would then remain there uneffaced, gradually crystallising itself, as it were, into a perfect shape ; and not till this process was attained was it put down on paper. His first transcription of his ideas took place early in the morning, after a very frugal breakfast, as he stood at his desk. The completion and instrumentation of all the various elements of an idea were undertaken in the evening. In his first sketch he generally noted down the voices fully, and only marked here and there the harmonies, or the places where the wind-instruments were to be introduced. Sometimes he indicated by signs, known only to himself, his most wonderful and characteristic orchestral effects. . . . The whole was already so firmly stereotyped upon his brain, that his instrumentation was little more than the labour of a copyist. . . .'[356] Concerning his opera *Der Freischütz*, Max says that Weber was much longer employed on the composition of this opera than on that of any other of his works. 'There is not a single piece of music in it,' declares Max von Weber, 'that he did not turn over twenty times in his mind, until he so felt it that he could say, "That's it!" and then he wrote it down rapidly, in a firm clear hand, almost without altering a note. . . .'[355] In his methods of working out his ideas Weber somewhat resembled Haydn who would put nothing down unless 'quite sure it was the right thing.' 'His practice,' Mr. Hadden says, 'was to sketch out his ideas roughly in the morning, and elaborate them in the afternoon, taking pains to preserve unity in idea and form.'[130]

There exists a very interesting letter from Balakirev to Tchaikovsky, which Mrs. Newmarch translates for her edition of Modeste Tchaikovsky's 'Life' of his famous brother Peter Ilich, which gives a vivid insight into his methods of composing an opera. 'I do not know your method of composing' writes Balakirev to Tchaikovsky, 'mine is as follows : when I wrote my *King Lear*, having first read the play, I felt inspired to compose an overture (which Stassov had already suggested to me). At first I had no actual material, I only warmed to the project. An Introduction, "maestoso,"

followed by something mystical (Kents' Prediction).   The
Introduction dies away and gives place to a stormy allegro.
This is Lear himself, the discrowned, but still mighty, lion.
By way of episodes the characteristic themes of Regan and
Goneril, and then—a second subject—Cordelia, calm and
tender.   The middle section (storm, Lear and the Fool on
the heath) and repetition of the allegro : Regan and Goneril
finally crush their father, and the overture dies away softly
(Lear over Cordelia's corpse), then the prediction of Kent is
heard once more, and finally the peaceful and solemn note
of death.   You must understand that, so far, I had no definite musical ideas.   These came later and took their place
within my framework.   I believe you will feel the same, if
once you are inspired by the project.   Then arm yourself
with goloshes and a walking-stick and go for a constitutional
on the Boulevards, starting with the Nikitsky ; let yourself
be saturated with your plan, and I am convinced by the
time you reach the Sretensky Boulevard some theme or
episode will have come to you.'[315]   Tchaikovsky himself has
given a very vivid account of his own methods of composing ;
most of this has already been quoted.   There is, however, a
letter to Frau von Meck which gives some further particulars.
He writes : 'You want to know my methods of composing?
Do you know, dear friend, that it is very difficult to give a
satisfactory answer to your question, because the circumstances under which a new work comes into the world vary
considerably in each case.

'First, I must divide my works into two categories, for this
is important in trying to explain my methods.   (1) Works
which I compose on my own initiative—that is to say, from
an invincible inward impulse.   (2) Works which are inspired by external circumstances : the wish of a friend, or a
publisher, and *commissioned* works.   Here I should add
experience has taught me that the intrinsic value of a work
has nothing to do with its place in one or the other of these
categories. . . . Works belonging to the first category do not
require the least effort of will.   It is only necessary to obey our
inward promptings, and if our material life does not crush
our artistic life under its weight of depressing circumstances,
the work progresses with inconceivable rapidity. . . .

'For the works in my second category it is necessary to *get into the mood*. To do so we are often obliged to fight with indolence and disinclination. . . . I consider it, however, the *duty* of an artist not to be conquered by circumstances. . . .

'Now I will try to describe my actual procedure in composition. . . . I usually write my sketches on the first piece of paper to hand. I jot them down in the most abbreviated form. A melody never stands alone, but invariably with the harmonies which belong to it. These two elements of music, together with the rhythm, must never be separated; every melodic idea brings its own inevitable harmony and its suitable rhythm. If the harmony is very intricate, I set down in the sketch a few details as to the working out of the parts; when the harmony is quite simple, I only put in the bass, or a figured bass, and sometimes not even this. If the sketch is intended for an orchestral work, the ideas appear ready-coloured by some special instrumental combination. The original plan of the instrumentation often undergoes some modifications. . . .'[318]

On the following day he writes again to Frau von Meck concerning the working out. This letter contains the following very significant statement: 'What has been set down in a moment of ardour must now be critically examined, improved, extended, or condensed, as the form requires.'[319]

It may now be of interest to turn to an English composer. Robert Buckley gives an account of Elgar's method in composing such a work as 'The Apostles.' Elgar said 'I first of all read everything I can lay my hands on which bears on the subject directly or indirectly, meditating on all that I have sifted out as likely to serve my purpose, and blending it with my musical conceptions. Every personality appears to me in a musical dress. I suppose that all who read novels form mental pictures of the characters. So with me: I involuntarily give to each a musical character, clothe each with a musical expression, in this case Judas, Peter, and the rest. I do not seek for character-motives: they come, in all places, at all seasons. I never sit down and say "Now I will compose." The thing is inconceivable to me. What comes, comes of itself; of course I am often thinking in music.'[27]

Music is written around a mood, is, in fact, the outcome of moods. What are the circumstances that set up the mood—in short what sort of things inspire musicians? For 'some match,' as Galsworthy says, 'must strike against the surface of their hearts and eyes.' Galsworthy was referring to literary artists, but it is all the same. Words have ever been a potent stimulus to musicians. Basil Maine translates a passage from the preface to Byrd's first book of *Gradualia* in which that composer shows plainly the almost magical power of words. 'There is in those very sentiments—as I have learned by experience—a mysterious hidden power, so that to anyone who considers carefully the divine mysteries and seriously ponders them in his heart, the most appropriate strains occur of their own accord in some strange way, and offer themselves copiously even when one's mind is sluggish and inactive.'[191] The fact is that the natural inflections of the voice when saying over words aloud or even mentally, suggest themes quite apart from the mood conveyed by the sense of the words. Also the subject of the words apart from the mood, sad or joyful, grave or gay, may influence the contour of the theme. Angels, for example, do not ascend to heaven on a downward scale but on an upward series of notes ; athletes do not run to slow long-drawn out notes, and so on. Words are especially provocative to musical inspiration since they provide so many different kinds of suggestions to the artist. Rimsky-Korsakoff relates how when he re-read *Snyegoorochka*, its wonderful poetic beauty dawned upon him and at once he longed to compose an opera on that subject. 'Immediately upon reading it. . .,' he says 'there began to come into my mind motives, themes, chord-passages, and there began to glimmer before me fleetingly at first, but more and more clearly later, the moods and clang-tints* corresponding to various movements of the subject.'[269] As we have seen, words had an astonishing effect upon Schubert, suggesting a song to him when he had only read a poem through twice. It is said that the old violinist-composer Tartini used to select some phrase from Petrarch before he began to compose, keeping the same in his mind as he worked. He used to write

* i.e. tone-colours.

these lines in cypher known only to himself, at the top of his manuscript.[147]

Nature is perhaps the most potent stimulus to inspiration but she sometimes affects musicians in a way that would not be expected. Schubert returned from a happy holiday in the Styrian Alps and set himself not to write a joyful song cycle, but to complete his mournful *Winterreise*. To Weber, the world appeared, as his son tells us, 'a world of tones.' Colour, form, space, time, were transformed into sounds. Lines and forms seem to have suggested melodies to him. His musical ideas came thickest when the sight of outward objects was accompanied by the rolling of carriage wheels, no doubt owing to the slightly hypnotic effect of the gentle rumbling. 'Melodies sprang from every rise or fall of the road' . . . 'Whenever any spot recurred to his memory, it was combined with the recollection of the melody it had inspired' . . . 'But it must not be supposed . . . that the nature of the outward objects,' says Max von Weber, 'always elicited analogous feelings. Sublime mountain scenery, by some strange chain of thought, or perhaps contrasting feeling, might give birth to a droll capriccio,— a joyous sunrise to a melancholy adagio,—a grotesque object to a grave motive. . . .'[355] Tchaikovsky notes the unconnectedness of musical works with daily life. 'Without any special reason for rejoicing,' he says, 'I may be moved by the most cheerful creative mood, and, *vice-versâ*, a work composed under the happiest surroundings may be touched with dark and gloomy colours.'[318] This is a phase of the creative mind that might profitably be investigated.

On one occasion when Charles Neate the pianist was walking with Beethoven in the fields near Barden talking of the wonderful way Beethoven had of representing pictures in music and speaking especially of his *Pastoral Symphony*, Beethoven confessed that he always had some picture in his mind when composing.[332] Mozart was much affected by nature : when travelling with his wife through beautiful scenery he would gaze earnestly upon the scene before him with grave and thoughtful expression. Presently his face would brighten and he would begin to hum the tunes that arose in his mind.[156] Country scenes were a great stimulus to

Scriabin, whose E flat *Prelude* in Opus II was suggested by the sight of a torrent flowing between great rocks it had perhaps torn asunder in its course.[153]

The musical mind catches at any likeness, however superficial, to music in the noises and objects of daily surroundings. To show the extent of these suggestions derived from ordinary objects we may cite the 'Laughing Chorus' in *Der Freischütz*, which owed its origin to the impression made on Weber by the false intoning of the responses in the Litany by some old women during an afternoon service in the Pillnitz Chapel.[355] A still more curious case of the musical mind reading musical analogies in everyday objects is illustrated by the account given by Max von Weber of the origin of the march in *Oberon*. 'Weber was accustomed, when performances took place at the "Linkesches Bad," to walk out after dinner and take his coffee there in the garden of the Elbe. One day a heavy rain had come on during the walk. . . . When he reached the garden, all the guests had been driven away by the rain, and the waiters had heaped the chairs and tables one upon another, with their legs sprawling in the air. The Capellmeister (*sic*) stood for a long time with his hands folded behind him gazing, at the grotesque groupings. . . . All on a sudden he called to young Roth, the clarionette-player (*sic*), who had been the companion of his walk, "Look there!" he said; "does not that look exactly like a great triumphal march? *Donnerwetter!* what chords there are for the trumpets! I can use that! I can use that!" He had just then been asked to compose a march for Gehe's tragedy of *Henry the Fourth*. Immediately on reaching home, after the theatre, Weber wrote down his singular inspiration, at first only for brass instruments. It was afterwards turned to account, and arranged for the orchestra in *Oberon*.'[355] It is easy to see how the chairs and tables piled on top of one another suggested great chords. To the musical mind always reading music into everything the solid table-tops and chair seats would suggest the heads of notes, whilst the upward and downward sprawling legs would suggest their tails; hence a pile of tables and chairs would represent chords.

PAINTING

Painters may be divided roughly into two groups : those who use nature to express their poetic dreams and those who approach nature scientifically, endeavouring to explore some new aspect and to paint this with the utmost faithfulness. Into the first group fall painters of historical subjects and of subject pictures in general and also certain landscape-painters. Their attitude towards the natural world will be similar to that of Delacroix, who said 'Nature is like a dictionary ; we look out our words in it, their derivation, their etymology, all the elements in fact that go to compose a sentence or a story, but no one has considered the dictionary as a composition in the poetical sense of the word. . . . Art is not an exact and literal transcription of Nature but a welding together by man's mind of elements found in Nature.'[32] This briefly is the attitude of poet-painters to nature. Some of the greatest landscape-painters have belonged to this group and their procedure bears as close an analogy to that of poets and novel-writers as the difference between their media will allow. A brief account of the procedure of some of these artists will show what it means to paint a picture from, as it were, the poetical standpoint. Beginning with Turner ; he studied nature by driving himself about in a gig sketching ; watching cloud effects, as he told Lady Millais, lying on his back in a boat 'gazing at the heavens for hours, and even days, till he had grasped some effect of light . . .'[215] that he wished to paint. In this wise Turner accumulated thousands of sketches and memoranda. His 'faculty of vision . . . ,' says Cyrus Redding, 'seemed to penetrate the sources of natural effect, however various in aspect, and to store them in memory with wonderful felicity. His glance commanded, in an instant, all that was novel in scenery, and a few outlines on paper recorded it unintelligibly to others. He placed these pictorial memoranda upon millboard, not larger than a sheet of letter paper. . . . His first sketches showed little of the after picture to the unpractised eye—perhaps he bore much away in memory, and these were a kind of short-hand which he deciphered in his studio.'[259] P. G. Hamerton states that as early as 1802, when Turner was only 27 years old, he already absolutely abandoned topographical fidelity and had, in fact, begun to paint his dreams. Hamerton arrived at this conclusion after visiting the scenes of many of Turner's pictures and comparing the picture with the actual scene. Turner travelled, Hamerton suggests, because he needed the stimulus of fresh scenes and places.[138] The effects he cared to paint were for the most part transient and his eagerness to search for new impressions prevented him from remaining long in one spot. The times given to his studies from nature must have varied, he suggests, from three to four minutes to as many hours;[140] and Turner made use of these pictorial memoranda with a poet's freedom.

There is a story which Hamerton relates that gives a further insight into this artist's methods. Turner was staying in a friend's house where there were three children. He had brought with him a drawing in which the distance was already filled in but there was no material for the nearer parts. One morning he called the children in to help him. Rubbing three cakes of water-colours, red, blue and yellow in three separate saucers, he gave one to each child and told them to dabble in the saucers and then play together with their coloured fingers on his paper. Turner watched earnestly for some time, then suddenly cried 'stop'! He took the drawing, added imaginary landscape suggested by the accidental colouring and then the picture was finished![141] Turner's colouring at times appears to have been symbolic. Thornbury points out that 'he was very definitely in the habit of indicating the association of any subject with the circumstances of death, especially the death of multitudes, by placing it under one of his most deeply crimsoned sunset skies.' For example: the storm-clouds above the *slave ship*; the clouds in *Ulysses and Polyphemus* and in the picture of *Napoleon at St. Helena* and in *The Old Téméraire*.[336] Probably many of his pictures were creations of his own mind whilst others were painted from memory of a vivid impression. Ruskin's *Dilecta* contains the story of the origin of Turner's picture, *Rain, Steam and Speed*, showing how Turner painted it from the vivid impression made upon him of what he saw when looking out of the train at Bristol.[274]

Thomas Gainsborough, W. B. Boulton says, painted little

direct from nature after his removal from Suffolk to Bath in
1760, and that in landscape his method 'is almost entirely
subjective, produced by the operation of his artistic understanding working with the material gathered in the fields
during the impressionable years of his student period.'[25]

Corot, we are told, used in early days to paint out of doors
but after a while he realised that his aim was to record an
impression and not to make an accurate copy of nature.[18]
He continued to make careful studies in order to learn the
language of nature and also to make notes for pictures he
wished to paint when he returned to his studio.   E. Meynell
relates how one day when Corot was sketching at Fontainebleau and had just finished a beautiful sketch in a quarter-of-
an-hour, he turned to *M.* Silvestre and said to him 'I will
make a picture from this, . . . but strictly speaking, I have
no need for it.   When I am asked for a replica of a landscape
I can make it without looking at the original.   I keep copies
of my works in my heart and in my eyes.   A landscape
painter should be able to paint a country masterpiece
without leaving Montmartre.'[213]   Another fragment of conversation preserved by Meynell gives a clear insight into
Corot's methods and that of poet-painters in general.
' "After my excursions," said he, "I invite friend Nature to
spend a few days under my roof ; and, she there, my fantasy
begins.   Brush in hand, I go forth into the woods of my
studio ; I hear birds sing there, and the trees rustle in a
phantom wind ; I see streams flowing, and my rivers are
charged with a thousand reflections of the sky and of everything upon their banks ; the sun sets and rises for me in my
home''.'[213]

Jean François Millet was able to produce effects of atmosphere, attitudes and gestures, from memory.   Miss Cartwright states that in later years he worked little from nature
herself as 'she does not pose.'   His ordinary practice was to
make small sketches of figures and landscapes indicating
the chief outlines and shadows and accentuating prominent
features.   'For instance,' she says, 'he would draw a group
of wheat-ricks in one of these little sketch-books, about two
and a half by three inches in size, carefully noting the shape
of the ricks, the sinking and bulging which were the result

of exposure to the weather, and from this rough pen-and-ink outline afterwards produce a complete and accurately-modelled picture.'[41]   Whistler's method with his nocturnal 'tone-poems' was to go out at night with a companion and stand before his subject and memorise it ; then he would turn his back upon the subject and repeat it to his companion until he knew it in its every detail.   The next morning if he could see upon his canvas the picture in its entirety he would begin to paint ; if not he would spend another night learning the subject off by heart.   Nature as he found her put Whistler out, he merely turned to her for inspiration.[243]

Studies made from Nature are merely looked upon as memoranda for the picture that is painted in the Studio ; at all events not in the direct presence of Nature.   'Studies made in the open air,' writes Van Gogh to his brother, 'are different from pictures that are destined to be brought before the public.   The latter, according to my opinion, result from studies, but yet they may or even must differ a great deal from them.   For in the picture the painter rather gives a personal idea, and in a study his aim is simply to analyse a bit of nature—either to make his idea or conception more correct, or to find a new idea.'[117]   Speaking of the possible sale of some of his studies, he says, 'We must not press the studies, which are more trouble to do but are less pleasing than the pictures which are the result and fruition of them, and which one paints as in a dream, with so much agonising.'[118]   And again he says, 'I am going to set myself to work from memory often, and the canvases from memory are always less awkward, and have a more artistic look than studies from nature, especially when one works in mistral weather.'[119]   There is, indeed, much to be said for painting from memory : Millet draws attention to the fact that one man may paint a picture from a careful drawing on the spot and another may paint the same scene from memory, from a brief but strong impression and that the picture made from memory may succeed better by giving the 'character and physiognomy' of the place though the details may be inexact.[41]   'I feel very certain,' Watts declared, 'that to render nature truly—that is, to give her inward beauty—one must make careful studies first, either in pencil or monochrome,

looking much and well at nature, and then coming
away and trying to paint the impression left on the mind.
For this reason I consider that the backgrounds in some of
Millais' pictures have far excelled the landscapes he painted
directly from nature.'[354]

The procedure of these poet-painters briefly is this : they
study Nature until they are saturated in her forms and
colours to the extent of being able to produce a convincing
figure-subject or landscape from memory.   They are able to
think in terms of Nature's forms and colours as the musician
is able to think in terms of notes and rhythm and the poet
in terms of words and rhythm.   Nothing can be done by
these artists without inspiration.   'Never paint . . . a subject,' said Corot, 'unless it calls insistently and distinctly upon
your eye and heart.'[212]   'We must feel deeply if we are to
paint at all,'[41] said Millet.   'Painting,' Constable declared, 'is
with me but another word for feeling. . . .'[179]   Their pictures
are not painted directly from Nature herself but only from
notes or a vivid impression carried in their mind.   Most of
the work is from memory.   This method allows time for the
inspiration to clear, and for insignificant details to sink away
leaving a vivid and sharp impression.   It is, in fact, the
poetic principle that emotion can only be expressed retrospectively, that is followed by these artists.

The scientific-painters, on the other hand, make it their
business to represent some new aspect of nature as faithfully
and accurately as possible.   Their wish is not to paint some
dream of their own but to paint Nature for her own sake.
Whereas the outlook of poetic-painters is subjective, the
outlook of scientific-painters is objective. ▸The object they
paint is Nature in some particular aspect.   The *result* may
be, and often is most beautiful and moving ; the method,
however, is rather that of a man of science accurately
observing and describing some object than that of a poet
brooding and dreaming.

One of the great moments in Ruskin's life was the day he
learnt to draw Nature as she is and to look at her, not as he
had done before, as Prout and Turner would have looked,
but through his own eyes.   One day he noticed, 'on the road
to Norwood, a bit of ivy round a thorn stem, which

seemed,' he said, 'even to my critical judgment, not ill composed.' Later in the same year (1842), when in the Forest of Fontainebleau he found himself 'lying on the bank of a cart-road in the sand, with no prospect whatever but a small aspen tree against the blue sky. Languidly, but not idly,' he says, 'I begin to draw it; and as I drew, the languor passed away: the beautiful lines insisted on being traced. . . . With wonder increasing every instant, I saw that they composed themselves by finer laws than any known of men. . .'[60]

Here indeed, was a great discovery: the beauty inherent in nature as she really is. Constable's method of working was a kind of half-way house between that of the poet-painters and scientific-painters. Leslie says, 'I remember to have heard him say, "when I sit down to make a sketch from Nature, the first thing I try to do is, *to forget that I have ever seen a picture*."' The aim of these scientific-artists is to paint what they *see* and not what they *know* to be there. One of Sargent's theories was that the painters of modern times show that they know too much about the substance they paint and that they ought to know nothing whatever about the nature of the object before them. Sargent's aim, says Charteris 'was to record with the utmost skill attainable the thing as he saw it, without troubling about its ethical significance, or, indeed, any significance other than its visual value.'[46]

Monet's method of procedure is typical of the scientific painter's outlook and is summarised here as an illustration. His object was to represent accurately one momentary phase or impression. The aspect of nature continually changes with the position of the sun, the clouds, the type of weather and the seasons. Monet's object was to catch one of these short phases and to paint it as accurately as possible. M. Duret says 'he begins to paint a landscape in the morning at sunrise, when the earth is covered with mist; he will note on canvas the reflected light that the rising sun throws over the landscape and the mist which enshrouds it. And, since he only paints any effect just so long as it actually exists before his eyes. . . . He will have to abandon it as soon as the sun has risen above the horizon.'[88]

For some time Monet varied the subject with the effect, but in 1890–91 he hit upon the idea of using the same subject and painting a series of impressions; sometimes as many as ten, twelve or fifteen on the same subject: for instance *Les Meules* and the series on the *Façade of Rouen Cathedral*.[88] The procedure, it will be noticed, differs fundamentally from that of the poet-painters since the picture is painted directly from nature herself and not at second hand from notes or from memory. The effect, or whatever it may be, is painted only so long as it lasts. The picture has no story to tell as such nor is the painter concerned with any value other than the visual. The scientific painting of light is one of the major contributions of these painters.

PORTRAITURE

There is little doubt that portraiture of the ordinary type is more nearly related to commercial art than to the fine arts of landscape and historical painting. Gainsborough, for instance, called his portrait work 'journeyman work in the face way.'[26] The success of a portrait depends very largely on the inspiration the artist derives from the sitter. For example, if Gainsborough's sitter was just an ordinary subject even he could only produce an uninspired work though competently and soundly painted. On the other hand, if the artist does find inspiration in his sitter the result is perhaps Bellini's 'Doge' or Gainsborough's 'Mrs. Siddons.' What it feels like to be painted when the artist *is* inspired is recorded by a sitter who inspired Sargent. She records her impressions thus: 'He was working at fever heat, and it was so infectious that I felt my temples throbbing in sympathy with his efforts, the veins swelling in my brow. At one moment I thought I was going to faint with the sense of tension and my fear to spoil the pose that enthused him.'[47]

The artist must overcome the personal resistance of his sitter and compel him to yield himself up in expression or gesture or he himself must be overcome by the personality of his sitter if the portrait is to be an inspired masterpiece.

Epstein makes this very significant statement concerning

portraiture [in bronze]: 'something very definitely passes between artist and model. It is always evident in a work when the artist has been bored or irritated with his model. It has happened in my experience more than once that some remark of my model has put me out of humour to such an extent that I have been unable to continue.'[93]

Sir Joshua Reynolds, we have seen, counselled his Academy students to pay especial attention to first thoughts since, as he says, 'There is in the commerce of life, as in Art, a sagacity which is far from being contradictory to right reason, and is superior to any occasional exercise of that faculty; which supersedes it: and does not wait for the slow process of deduction, but goes at once, by what appears a kind of intuition, to the conclusion. A man endowed with this faculty, feels and acknowledges the truth, though it is not always in his power, perhaps, to give a reason for it. . . .'[264] This faculty is ordinarily known as the power of feeling, one might say the power of the knowledge of feeling, since it is as Sir Joshua Reynolds says, 'the result of the accumulated experience of our whole life.'[264] Therefore the feeling giving rise to first thoughts on any artistic subject should receive particular attention. Blake said: 'First thoughts are best in art, second thoughts in other matters.'[115] Reynolds has one more word of counsel: We are not to neglect the good fortune that may come unsolicited. 'Accident,' he says, 'in the hands of an artist who knows how to take advantage of its hints, will often produce bold and capricious beauties of handling. . . . Works produced in an accidental manner will have the same free unrestrained air as the works of nature. . . .'[263] And finally, Blake adds a word of warning: 'Do you work in fear and trembling?. . .' 'Indeed I do Sir.' 'Then you'll do,' said Blake.[115]

SCIENTIFIC RESEARCH

It is the business of the scientist to discover and explain some part of the mechanism of nature. In order to do this he has to observe and record facts and to interpret the facts when collected. There may come a point when he has much the same feeling that a child has upon turning out the pieces of a jig-saw puzzle. He may find himself as it were fitting a piece of sky into the sea or a piece of tree-top into a hedge in the foreground of the picture. When facts are in this chaotic jumble it is here that the 'instrument of feeling' will be of the greatest importance. If the scientist has, during the whole of his life, observed carefully, trained himself to be on the look-out for analogy and possessed himself of relevant knowledge, then the 'instrument of feeling,' being as Sir Joshua Reynolds said 'the result of the accumulated experience of our whole life,' will become a powerful divining rod leading the scientist to discover order in the midst of chaos by providing him with a clue, a hint, or an hypothesis upon which to base his experiments. This clue or hypothesis is the inspiration of the man of science; and this power of divination one of the characteristics of his genius. S. P. Thompson speaks of the power of divination of Lord Kelvin: 'Often he had to labour to devise explanations of that which had so come to him; and instances are known of his spending whole days upon trying to frame or recover a demonstration of something that had been previously obvious to him.' Thompson states further that it is not without significance that in the sentence in which Lord Kelvin stated his inability to accept the 'Darwinian hypothesis of natural selection he should have said: "I have *felt* that this hypothesis does not contain the true theory of evolution." '[334] Reiser says of Einstein 'His entire working procedure is surprisingly analogous to that of the artist. Once he has come upon a problem, his path toward solution is not a matter of slow, painful stages. He has a definite vision of the possible solution, and considers its value and the methods of approaching it. . . .'[261]

It will be seen that in what we may call creative science, feeling plays a leading part. Facts are collected, feeling suggests a theory of interpretation; it is then that reason comes into play in devising experiments or further observation to check the theory feeling has suggested. In fact, feeling in Sir Joshua Reynolds' sense plays a leading part in every type of creative thought.

Charles Darwin used to say that 'no one could be a good observer unless he was an active theoriser.'[68]   It may happen that the mind is quick as in the case of Darwin to sense analogies and to formulate theories. If the theory is a good one the thinker is in danger of being fascinated by it to the extent of unknowingly shutting his eyes to anything that may negative it. On the other hand the true investigator will keep on the look out for exceptions. Sir Francis Darwin writing of his father says:

'There was one quality of mind which seemed to be of special and extreme advantage in leading him to make discoveries. It was the power of never letting exceptions pass unnoticed. Everybody notices a fact as an exception when it is striking or frequent, but he had a special instinct for arresting an exception. A point apparently slight and unconnected with his present work is passed over by many a man almost unconsciously with some half-considered explanation, which is in fact no explanation. It was just these things that he seized on to make a start from.'[68]

Sir J. J. Thomson considers that teaching should be combined with research since there is no better way of getting a grasp of the subject, or more likely to start ideas for research, than teaching or lecturing about it; and if your hearers are a little stupid all the better.[335]

When problems arise it would seem the best thing to make sure exactly what the nature of the problem is and, further, to make clear what sort of a solution is expected and to put this in writing. Then, following the general procedure in such cases, it is usually best to put the subject aside for a while.

Visualizing or making a mental image of a problem would appear to be a good plan. Thinking in words is apt in some cases to be cramping. Sir Francis Galton says: 'Latterly' [1887] . . . 'I had some common arithmetic series to sum, and worked them out, not by the use of the formula, but by the process through which the formula is calculated, and that without the necessity of any mental word. . . . In simple geometry I always work with actual or mental lines; in fact I fail to arrive at the full conviction that a problem is fairly taken in by me, unless I have contrived somehow to disembarrass it of words. . . .'[107] The trouble about thinking without words is the difficulty of expressing the discovery in an intelligible form afterwards. Galton says: 'It is a serious drawback to me in writing, and still more in explaining myself, that I do not so easily think in words as otherwise. It often happens that after being hard at work, and having arrived at results that are perfectly clear and satisfactory to myself, when I try to express them in language I feel that I must begin by putting myself upon quite another intellectual plane. I have to translate my thoughts into a language that does not run very evenly with them. I therefore waste a vast deal of time in seeking for appropriate words and phrases, and am conscious, when required to speak on a sudden, of being often very obscure through mere verbal maladroitness, and not through want of clearness of perception. This is one of the small annoyances of my life. I may add that often while engaged in thinking out something I catch an accompaniment of nonsense words, just as the notes of a song might accompany thought. Also, that *after* I have made a mental step, the appropriate word frequently follows as an echo; as a rule, it does not accompany it.'

'Lastly I frequently employ nonsense words as temporary symbols, as the logical x and y of ordinary thought, which is a practice that, as may well be conceived, does not conduce to clearness of exposition.'[107] It is probable that Clerk Maxwell also thought without words. We are told that he used to make a mental image of every problem:[34] also that when young 'His replies in ordinary conversation were indirect and enigmatical,'[35] and that when first he began to lecture [*Æt.* 25] he was sometimes led to make 'chaotic statements.' The 'family trick of "calling things out of their names",'[36] further supports the view that most of his thinking may have been done without the use of words or with nonsense words as was the case with Galton. Would that we had a language such as that described by Swedenborg as the language of Heaven where writings 'flow naturally from the thoughts themselves . . . as if thought puts itself forth; nor does the hand pause for the choice of a word, because the words which they speak as well as those which they write correspond to the ideas of their thought. . . .'³¹⁰ While on the subject of writing, it may be noted that Joseph Priestley usually wrote his works in shorthand; transcribing in longhand what he had written in shorthand the day before.²⁵⁴

The mechanical procedure, i.e. note-taking and writing for a great theoretical work is always a matter of interest; we therefore conclude with Darwin's own account of his methods :—

'There seems,' he says, 'to be a sort of fatality in my mind leading me to put at first my statement or proposition in a wrong or awkward form. Formerly I used to think about my sentences before writing them down; but for several years I have found that it saves time to scribble in a vile hand, whole pages as quickly as I possibly can, contracting half the words; and then correct deliberately. Sentences thus scribbled down are often better ones than I could have written deliberately.

'Having said thus much about my manner of writing, I will add that with my large books I spend a good deal of time over the general arrangement of the matter. I first make the rudest outline in two or three pages, and then a larger one in several pages, a few words or one word standing for a whole discussion or series of facts. Each one of these headings is again enlarged and often transferred before I begin to write *in extenso*. As in several of my books, facts observed by others have been very extensively used, and as I have always had several quite distinct subjects in hand at the same time, I may mention that I keep from thirty to forty large portfolios, in cabinets with labelled shelves, into which I can at once put a detached reference or memorandum. I have bought many books, and at their ends I make an index of all the facts that concern my work; or, if the book is not my own, write out a separate abstract, and of such abstracts I have a large drawer full. Before beginning on any subject I look to all the short indexes and make a general and classified index, and by taking the one or more proper portfolios I have all the information collected during my life ready for use.'⁶⁶

CHAPTER VI

CONCLUSION

The foregoing five chapters were intended to present inspiration as it appears and as it is experienced : the preparation and also the way in which inspiration is treated in general, together with the special procedure for the novel, poetry, music, painting and scientific research.

The first chapter, dealing with the preparation, stressed the fact that before anyone could give himself up to inspiration he must have acquired a mastery over his subject in order that the technical aspect should be in no way a hindrance to him. Another point of great importance to which attention was called is that new discoveries and inventions resulting, as they frequently do, from the coalition of ideas gathered from widely different subjects, knowledge outside and beyond the chosen profession is a considerable asset towards the achievement of the new and original. It was shown that some persons who attained distinction in later life practised their vocation from childhood ; and that their general standard of culture was as a rule unusually wide. For example, Goethe found time to interest himself in Science and in the engineering operations of canal, tunnel and harbour building. James Watt would rest his mind from the problems of the steam engine and double condensation, in metaphysics and in archaeology and poetry.

The second chapter showed the appearance of inspiration in relation to the creative mind in arts and sciences. In creative thought we get two main types of inspiration. On the one hand ideas more or less clear cut, as the themes of a sonata, a stanza of poetry, the solution of a problem. But on the other hand, inspiration may arise in the form of an impression as the 'vague notion of a plot' for a novel or the visions of pictures which flashed up in the mind of Van Gogh as 'in a dream' when he was wandering about in the sunny fields. Or again the 'feeling' of something : a kind of affective impression as when Stevenson wrote *The Merry Men*, beginning with the 'feeling' of a certain island. It should be noted in passing that the meaning of an inspiration is not always understood by the recipient, though in many cases it may seem to him only just to be out of reach. For example, William James writes to his wife of an experience on the 'slopes of Mt. Marcy' :—

'I spent a good deal of it (i.e. the night) in the woods, where the streaming moonlight lit up things in magical checkered play, and it seemed as if the Gods of all the nature-mythologies were holding an indescribable meeting in my breast with the moral Gods of the inner life. . . . The intense significance of some sort, of the whole scene, if one could only *tell* the significance; the intense inhuman remoteness of its inner life, and yet the intense *appeal* of it; its everlasting freshness and its immemorial antiquity and decay; . . . In point of fact, I can't find a single word for all that significance, and don't know what it was significant of, so there it remains, a mere boulder of *impression*. Doubtless in more ways than one, though, things in the Edinburgh lectures will be traceable to it.'[245]

It does not matter, however, to the creative mind, if the significance is *not* understood provided the recipient can *do* something with his inspiration. An artist, understanding no more than James, could have painted the scene and it is also probable that musicians may experience impressions which they could not define in words but could express in music.

Whichever form the inspiration takes it comes unsought as a gift without any kind of effort at the time on the part of the recipient. In our opinion therefore an idea or an impression which comes into the mind without effort is an inspiration irrespective of its triviality or value. Usually, however, ideas and impressions arising in this way are accompanied with the sense of their value. Or it may well be that only those which are thus accompanied are taken account of. Although inspiration is an automatism and arises without effort it may give rise to intense action. This action is often accompanied as Parry told us with vitality almost supernatural. On the other hand it may give rise to no more than the state of deep concentration.* For

* F. Paulhan says: "extreme concentration is usually accompanied, so far as I am able to judge, by a kind of emotion—" (*The Laws of Feeling*, English translation by C. K. Ogden, London: Kegan Paul, Trench, Trubner & Co., 1930, p. 50).

example, Leslie records no great emotional tension of Constable when painting but merely that he sat very still, so still that once a field mouse crept into his pocket.[180]

The expressions used to describe inspiration : 'this magic process,' 'this supernatural and inexplicable force,' convey the sense of mystery and even of awe. As we have seen, the recipient feels himself to be possessed by some power whilst he is nothing but its mouth-piece or instrument. Gathering up some of the statements concerning this from the quotations cited we find remarks such as these : 'When I am in labour with a book I don't quite know what happens'— 'Some beneficent power shows it to me.' 'The feeling of being a receiver, an instrument, a mouth-piece has always been so strong in me.' 'The wind blows my old harp as it lists.'

As an exception to the sense of awe excited by inspiration we noted that certain men of genius disclaimed or mistrusted it. Constable, it will be remembered, rebuked Blake for using the term in connexion with one of his studies. Sir Joshua Reynolds evidently considered the cause of inspiration to be nothing more than hard work combined with the study of the great old masters. Flaubert and Rodin went further and issued a warning against it. A possible explanation may be found in the fact that inspiration had been too often identified by its 'enthusiasm' : a condition which could be induced artificially.

Chapter III outlined the general procedure of those who experience inspiration whether in art or in science. Here was shown that the conditions most favourable on the whole were 'half-sleep,' the state between sleeping and waking deepening at times into trance ; and lying in bed in the morning or at night. Quietness was not deemed essential but peace of mind and freedom from sudden interruptions or noises was considered necessary. Two methods of procedure were noted and these were total absorption in one piece of work until its completion on the one hand ; whilst on the other, a number of different things were worked at more or less concurrently. In the arts, the general procedure was to leave a pause between the inspiring influence and the work in order to allow the inspiration time to clear itself from irrelevant matters.

Another important feature of the general procedure is the checking and proving of inspirational ideas afterwards in the light of calm judgment. The reason for this is that whereas on the one hand inspirational ideas cannot be regarded in themselves as true or false since they comprise any idea irrespective of truth or falsity which wells up in the mind without effort as a gift; on the other hand, the value assigned to them by the mind may be erroneous. Poincaré is the only one so far as we know who has definitely referred to this phenomenon though knowledge of it is implied by Tchaikovsky, Rogers, Pasteur and others who have insisted on the necessity of checking. It should be noted also as an interesting exception to general experience that Poincaré found that this deceptive sense of value was most likely to occur in relation to ideas that came to him in the morning or at night when he was in bed in a semi-somnolent state.

The evanescence of inspirational ideas and impressions is another curious fact. At the time these appear sharp and clear, impossible to forget, in fact, indelibly etched on the mind; yet every poet and musician knows that if the themes or verses are not put down at once they will fade out within a few hours never to be recovered; in this respect they are like a vivid dream forgotten on waking.

The state of inspiration is not directly under the control of the will. No one can say 'now I will be inspired.' The more he strives the less likely is he to succeed; in fact, the only effort allowed by 'the Rules' is patient, regular work with the view of tuning in the mind to receive it. But inspiration may also be coaxed in other ways, such as by working in artificial light, taking up the pen in readiness to begin, and so on. Absence of effort, passiveness and receptiveness were shown to be essential conditions of mind; in fact, inspiration flourishes in a kind of looking-glass land in which everything appears to go contrary to the accepted notions of common sense. Great and valuable ideas are more likely to occur when the mind is half asleep than when it is fully awake; and the more a man strives the less is he likely to achieve, for the decisive idea has the way of appearing when the mind is passive and even contemplating nothing in particular. In fact Lewis Carroll's account of the creation of 'Alice' sums up much that we have attempted to make clear. 'In writing it out,' he says, 'I added many fresh ideas which seemed to grow of themselves upon the original stock;* and more added themselves when, years afterwards I wrote it all over again for publication: but (this may perhaps interest some readers of "Alice" to know) every such idea, and nearly every word of the dialogue, *came of itself*. Sometimes an idea comes at night, when I have had to get up and strike a light to note it down— sometimes when out on a lonely winter walk, when I have had to stop, and with half frozen fingers jot down a few words which should keep the new-born idea from perishing —but, whenever or however it comes, *it comes of itself*. I cannot set invention going like a clock, by any voluntary winding-up: nor do I believe that any *original* writing (and what other writing is worth preserving?) was ever so produced.'[40A]

Chapters IV and V in their various sections attempted to show the special procedure for arts and sciences. From this we learnt that Inspiration does not continue long. Tchaikovsky declared that if it lasted long without intermission no artist would survive it.

In the arts, as we have seen, inspiration may give as much as the themes and general structure of a symphony; even at times a complete short poem or a song; and on the other hand it may provide as little as the nucleus of one word or a short phrase from which a poem is developed; some of Tennyson's poems arose in this way. Or it may give no more than the vague notion of the plot and the sentence which the novel ends as with Daudet's *Rois en Exil*; or it may diffuse some rare feeling or emotion. Stevenson's story *The Merry Men* arose, it will be remembered, from 'the feeling' of an island on the west coast of Scotland. Whatever the inspiration gives be it great or little the effect on the artist is profound because it provides the very foundation of his work from

---

* Wyndham Lewis said: 'a work of art is a sort of animal—it is not easy for me to tell you just how it is made. It grows all sorts of things on itself—for effect—as it goes along.'[222D]

which the superstructure is developed almost mechanically : though the artist may not know where he is being led or what new realm he is destined to discover. The main function of inspiration in artistic work is, therefore, to provide the nucleus from which the work develops.

The origin of the inspirational nucleus of a work of art is a very difficult problem. Alphonse Daudet's views appear, however, to shed some light on this matter. His son Léon tells us that the 'problem of the beginning of a work and of the earliest spark of suggestion' occupied them very often. His father, he says, believed 'that in the case of all creators there are accumulations of sentient force made without their knowledge. Their nerves, in a state of high excitation, register visions, colors, forms, and odors in those half-realized reservoirs which are the treasuries of poets. All of a sudden, through some influence or emotion, through some accident of thought, these impressions meet each other with the suddenness of a chemical combination.'[73] This statement, that something is required to discharge the sentient force before the inspiration can arise, is interesting, as it is borne out by Galsworthy, who said of writers 'some match must strike against the surface of their hearts or eyes.' The arts, as we saw, are built up around moods and once the match is struck ideas, similes, visions relevant to these moods rush together to be poured out molten into words, notes or colours. It is interesting that Byron should have said 'All convulsions end with me in rhyme;' . . .[220]

The main function of inspiration in scientific work is to provide the solutions to problems. And in fact, one of the most remarkable phases, the flash of intuition, is particularly associated with the solution of scientific and mechanical problems. This solution is attributed by some to the mysterious workings of the subconscious mind. A problem arises and cannot be solved. The scientist, to rest himself, turns to something else, and apparently forgets his problem ; one day when perhaps he is crossing the street or stepping into a 'bus, and not thinking over the subject at all or even

considering some other matter the solution comes suddenly
to him.   The subconscious mind is supposed to have
provided the solution during the period of rest.*   We do not
believe that the subconscious mind provides the solution by
itself.   In the first place the subconscious mind can only
provide the solution if the necessary ideas are already stored
within the mind† ; and secondly it is far from likely that a
problem in an important piece of scientific work could be set
aside and entirely forgotten.   The following theory presents
itself as more probable.   The eye when focussed on some
particular point in a landscape takes in an area beyond the
actual point on which it is trained.   For instance, a man
might focus his eyes upon a church and then turn them
slightly and focus them on a neighbouring mansion in such a
way that he still could see the church out of the corner of his
eye while actually looking at the house.   Much the same
sort of thing appears to happen in the 'landscape' of the field
of consciousness.   The man whom we supposed to be gazing
at the mansion is not aware of the objects on the fringe of
vision ; he has probably forgotten the church in his interest
in the mansion ; but the whole of the field of vision is present
to his conscious mind.   It is likely that when the mind
turns away from a problem and focusses on some other
object, that the problem remains in the field of consciousness
in the same way as the church and other objects remained
within the field of vision of the man who was looking at the
great house.   It is suggested, therefore, that the problem is
not forgotten but merely set aside ; and that it is not rele-
gated to the depths of the subconscious mind.   This holding
the problem in the corner of the mind's eye while focussing
on something else not only rests the brain but sets it to
catch anything which will either solve or give the hint of the
solution.   When a problem arises there is naturally some
dim or vague notion of the type of solution required.   And
when we say the mind is set to catch at any idea which may
give the clue to the solution, we mean that it is ready to

* See Montmasson (Joseph—Marie), *Invention and the Unconscious*,
translated by H. Stafford Hatfield, London: Kegan, Paul, Trench,
Trubner & Co, 1931, p. 1.

† See Dr. C. Spearman, *Creative Mind*, London: Nisbet & Co., 1930,
pp. 76–77.

pounce upon any ideas bearing upon the type of solution required.

The ideas providing the desired hint, or, in other words, providing the flash of intuition can only arise by means of (1) a fortuitous combination of ideas already within the mind or, (2) by some external factor heard or seen.

The mechanism governing the chance combination of ideas which we now propose has already been referred to by the author in an earlier work,[142] in which attention was called to the possibility of ideas bearing on interests acquiring a certain tone which binds them together and also enables the mind to distinguish one interest from another. This tone appears also to act as a sieve preventing incongruous and irrelevant ideas from disturbing the mind. The ideas forming the interest, which are of course those directly applicable to it, tend, nevertheless, to become crusted over with other ideas not applicable to the interest, or to any idea comprising it, by a kind of interest association. For example, a man may be a keen racing-motorist but his ideas concerning the technique of driving on a certain track may bring with them also the vision of faces staring at him from the grand-stand and other irrelevant matters which he happened to notice when racing. These interest associations form a periphery of ideas attached to the interest which we have called elsewhere fringe-ideas[142] and acquire a similar tone on that account. Since they have acquired a similar tone they tend to become available together with the ideas forming the interest itself. When the thinker is awake these apparently irrelevant fringe-ideas will probably be ignored because judgment is in full play, but as the psychoanalysts insist, in the half-waking and related states, ordinary inhibitory functions are weakened and judgment is suspended so that realms of mind which are ordinarily kept apart may come together. It is here that the subconscious mind comes in. By the very inconsequence of its association during sleep or half-sleep one of the fringe-ideas ordinarily ignored may suddenly penetrate to the threshold of the conscious mind and it may be the decisive one which is required. It is also possible that two entirely different interests may have fringe-ideas in common or so nearly alike in tone that the mind may be led imperceptibly through several different interests by their mutually related fringe-ideas until the solution is arrived at.

When the mind does not contain the materials for the solution no amount of subconscious (or conscious) work will provide it ; therefore some other factor must be involved. This will be some external factor accidentally met with. The scientist, baffled by his problem, comes across some external factor which gives rise to the flash of intuition. This may be something he reads or notices or happens to see on a walk, etc. He may not be aware of what it is that has given rise to his so-called flash of intuition, but there are a number of instances in which the factor giving the clue has been noted. Here are two examples :

(1) John Bernoulli, the best-known mathematician of his day, was working on the geometry of falling bodies. He issued a problem broadcast to all the geometers in Europe as a challenge to them to solve it. Newton received a copy. He examined the problem on his return one day from the Mint, and before he went to bed that night he had not only solved the problem but generalised the result.[308] How did he arrive at the solution? We know how it was because Newton's friend, Dr. William Stukeley, relates the following incident which occurred on April 15th, 1726.

'After dinner, the weather being warm, we went into the garden and drank thea, under the shade of some appletrees, only he and myself. Amidst other discourse, he told me, he was just in the same situation, as when formerly, the notion of gravitation came into his mind. It was occasion'd by the fall of an apple, as he sat in contemplative mood. Why should that apple always descend perpendicularly to the ground, thought he to him self. Why should it not go sideways or upwards, but constantly to the earths centre? Assuredly, the reason is, that the earth draws it. There must be a drawing power in matter: and the sum of the drawing power in the matter of the earth must be in the earths center, not in any side of the earth. Therefore dos this apple fall perpendicularly, or towards the center. If matter thus draws matter, it must be in proportion of its quantity. Therefore the apple draws the earth, as well as the earth draws the apple. That there is a power, like that we here call gravity, which extends its self thro' the universe.

'And thus by degrees he began to apply this property of gravitation to the motion of the earth and of the heavenly bodys. . . . '309

(2) A. R. Wallace describes the effect of an external factor in leading himself and Darwin to their famous theory of evolution by survival of the fittest. He says :—

'Finally both Darwin and myself, at the critical period when our minds were freshly stored with a considerable body of personal observation and reflection bearing upon the problem to be solved, had our attention directed to the system of *positive checks* as expounded by Malthus in his "Principles of Population." The effect of that was analogous to that of friction upon the specially prepared match, producing that flash of insight which led us immediately to the simple but universal law of the "survival of the fittest".'195*

We have seen that the simile of the match striking upon a prepared surface was also used by Galsworthy. Probably Galsworthy, who had scientific interests, may have read this well-known passage and forgotten that he had read it, but it is none the less significant that he should have used this simile to illustrate the origin of inspiration in the art of literature. The fact is the principle underlying inspiration in the arts and in science is the same. The mind of the artist emotionally charged meets accidentally with something which 'strikes against the surface of his heart or eye' and a flash of inspiration results. On the other hand a new scientific theory comes into being or a new discovery or invention is made at that point when the investigator's mind, primed up with facts and by reflection on them, pent up in the unsuccessful attempt to solve a problem, meets accidentally with some external factor which provides a clue to the solution of his problem. The match is struck and light follows. The part played by accident or chance is therefore of great importance in creative thought. In science when a problem cannot be solved by any of the ordinary methods it is something accidentally met with

---

* Malthus, in this quotation, was the 'something accidentally met with' which provided Darwin, when his mind was already primed with a considerable amount of information, with the hypothesis on which to work. Wallace had read Malthus many years before and it was the recollection of it in 1858 which led to his solution.

which supplies as it were the missing keystone to the arch. In the arts, when the mind is primed up with what Daudet calls 'sentient force,' it is again something accidentally met with that discharges this and gives rise to the flash of inspiration.

Inspiration may thus be defined as the result of some unknown factor accidentally met with operating on the mind of the man of science or artist at that particular moment when it is pent up to a certain tension either by accumulation of 'visions, colours, forms,' or by facts and pondering over them in the unsuccessful attempt to solve a problem.   Although inspiration can occur to anyone it will only be manifested in its highest degree in those persons who are capable of this emotional tension.

Inspiration places the recipient for the time being into a phase of existence different from that of his everyday world because in working out his theories or in the pursuit of his artistic creation his own wishes and desires are overruled by his knowledge of natural sequences of events, colours, forms, rhythms, tones.   This may be summed up by saying he follows and *must* follow where the truth leads him.   Of course it is obvious and has long been recognised in the case of scientific discovery that truth alone must be followed, but truth is followed to the same degree in all great art.   We have seen in the Introductory section and Chapter IV that the realm of the imagination being founded in Nature is also subject to laws.   For example, a convincing character in a novel is one with whom we feel we could converse ; someone who lives and breathes as we do.   It was seen how Barrie refused to alter the end of *A Window in Thrums*, painful though it was to him, because the sad ending was more natural than a happy ending would have been.   Balzac, when begged to save some wild young man or unhappy woman, replied 'Truth above all . . . what happens to them is inevitable.'   In music the notes of a melody and the accompaniment must follow naturally.   The chords may be new and strange but they may follow each other in natural succession none the less.   Every musician knows when harmonies are forced and unnatural.   Even a fictitious monster such as a dragon strikes terror only in relation to its naturalness ; it must give the illusion at least that its limbs could move and its tail lash. Although the Poet, as Sidney said, 'lifted up with the vigour of his owne invention, doth grow in effect, another nature,' yet he never forgets his true mistress, Nature herself, and ever 'goeth hand in hand' with her. The truly inspired person achieves therefore a kind of mystic union with the natural world. And since he has for the time being achieved this union, all he has then to do, as Tchaikovsky says, is to follow his 'inward promptings.' He may well say, therefore, that 'some beneficent power' shows it to him and that he himself does not invent it. The strange utterances of those inspired persons who referred to a mystic possession of themselves when creating, as the 'not herself' of George Eliot and 'the other' of George Sand, are not after all as fantastic as at first they appeared when allowance is made for a little poetic licence ; for we are now in the position to name these mysterious agents : Nature who exerts her sway over all lovers of the truth and the unseen hands of chance and accident.

SUNRISE POEM

THE sun, a serene and ancient poet,
Stoops and writes on the sunrise sea
In softly undulant cyphers of gold
Words of Arabian charactery;
And the lovely riddle is lovingly rolled
With sound of slumberous, peaceful thunder
Around the sky and the sea thereunder
Toward my feet.   What is here enscrolled?
Is it poem or a story?
I cannot command this charactery,
But I think it is both and that it reads
This glorious morning as of old
When the first sun rose above the first sea,
As read it will while there is sea
And sun to scribe with quill of gold.
It is both story and a poem,
A hymn as also a history
Concerning the mightiest of mages,
The best that has been or shall be
Writ for any throughout the ages,
Writ for any, whoever he be
Or the most scholarly of sages
Or the most awkward of those who plod,
For Greek, Jew, Infidel and Turk—
As it was written too for me—
One page, two eternal sentences:
'The Heavens declare the Glory of God
And the Firmament showeth His Handiwork.'

Appendix

BIRTH OF A POEM

BY

Robert Nichols

She must have anchored in the small hours. For I remember being sensible of a change in the way she rolled—a beautiful easy roll that had something accomplished and elegant about it —before I sank into sleep again. It was by no means a normal sleep. I was exhausted by the pains of a duodenal ulcer and several days and nights of more or less continuous poetical composition. Never had I had such a 'run' of poetry. Scarcely did I feel my hook well into one poem and was playing to land it whole, fresh and silvery, than another would get onto the line. I had, it appeared, chanced into a portion of the earth's surface where the quality of light, which in my case tends to produce what Schiller calls 'the musical mood,' was uncommonly frequent and where every object that solicited eye or ear was altogether exceptionally charged with significance—a significance which, whatever its value for other poets, was to me so extreme that I felt not so much as if these objects had always been waiting for some poet to turn up and give them voice, as that they had been always waiting for me rather than any other. For while it is true that when the poet is in 'the musical mood' almost everything he sees and hears solicits his voice, yet there are areas in which the objects are both of a more instant and intense poetical potentiality than he is like to find elsewhere and recognisable by him as being in some recondite manner peculiarly his.* I was now in such an area and not only was the light by which the existence of these significances could be descried more continuous than I had ever known it but the riches existed in greater profusion, and I myself, detached from past and future, was in a condition in which any pause of partial deafness and blindness, however desirable as a means of rest, was seemingly become impossible.

Five days before—was it?—I'd lost count of time!—I had gone ashore at Madeira and the 'run' of poetry had started. Then we had touched at one of the Canary Islands—Teneriffe perhaps?—and now we were due at Las Palmas in the Grand Canaries. Talk about the lucid insanity of a fit of gambling! of following a rolling red ball or a dancing figure! Already

---

* It is as if he came into the native country of his soul, which may well be the *opposite* of that he has physically inhabited. Tennyson, a master of *distance* and brought up in the Fens, comes to himself in the Pyrenees.

I dared not lift eye from the notebook in which I scribbled, largely, alas, illegibly (as I was later to find) during my wanderings. These wanderings had little method. They were the zigzags of attraction and evasion. For the world had become an open Book, the seals of which had been broken, the pages of which blew this way and that as if fluttered by a wind whose passage I could not feel. And on every page a symbol clamoured to impart its significance. Consider a state of being in which it has become apparent that the vast conspiracy of the mystery of things has been annulled as by a silent proclamation issued overnight, a state of being in which you have but to lift your eyes to apprehend with entire ease the latent meaning of whatever catches your eye, a meaning which you cannot but read whether you will or no! Try to imagine a situation in which you were suddenly to become aware that the age of wisdom had dawned and was to be understood as established for an undetermined number of minutes, hours or days during which your heart was permitted to enter into the life of every particular it beheld! I remember a hummingbird, a flower, a silvery wall and a palladian tower above the wall. On which should I let my eye linger? Which would impart the most? Obviously a choice was imposed. For flesh, blood and faculties couldn't stand up to this incessant battering of significances. And yet, save the eye dwelled awhile on each, how was one to estimate how much bird or flower or silvery wall or tower promised?

I was distressingly aware that I was making very far from all I ought theoretically to have been making of this staggering opportunity, which might at any moment no longer be mine whether by reason of exhaustion or because the Book might be suddenly closed. Confusion was increasing as the rate of reception quickened. I had more than I could handle and still the essence of the seen and heard came pouring in.

I wished to get back to the ship and the isolation of the waters surrounding her. I pictured to myself the solitude and longed-for solidity of my little cabin with my dressing-gown sidling upon the wall and the loneliness of the pure, empty and perfect sky shining in the port-hole. Even that light, I reflected, could be partially shut out and, having screened it, I could lie in demi-obscurity while I disentagled the web of scrawls in my notebook.

I found myself on a dusty road and searched in vain for some conveyance to bear me to the quay. There wasn't a vehicle in sight. So I wandered through a deserted overgrown garden onto the nearby shore, where the small waves were falling with a low, regular, thumping sound along sands of a curious colour—rose-madder, dusted with lavender. Seaward a whitish vapour overhung the sweltering, restless wilderness, shutting out the horizon and giving the whole prospect a hushed, muffled and slightly sinister air. Behind me rose a derelict, clapboarded house. Broken Venetian blinds sagged in the dark empty window-spaces and a mop of bougainvillaea slid slipshod from the roof.

My hope was that the sound and spectacle of the sea might drug and drown further reception.

A vain hope! As each wave crumbled up those sands, I was sensible of age and sorrow seeking to express itself in a series of abrupt and heavy sighs. Puzzled, I glanced at the house and perceived that it wasn't a house but a head. This head had the worn face of a woman of about twenty-eight. Evidently she had stumbled into much tribulation and wasn't out of it yet. There was, apparently, nothing the poor creature could do about her *trouble*—except, of course, unburden to me. The sea flounced. 'I was talking to you. . . . Hey, you, Mister.' It sighed impatiently, shook itself, gathered its griefs, and resumed its rhythm. As for me, I kept my eyes fixed on the patch of sand immediately about my feet. But the house-which-was-a-woman had stolen up behind me and was breathing in my ear. 'It's not exactly what you might call plain murder,' she mourned 'but if you leave a person or a house to die. . . .' And yet one couldn't assert that she said this in so many words. She wasn't talking prose. There was no short-story there save by implication. No; another poem, the sixth that morning! And none of them completed!

I made my way back to the road, found a broken-down fly, reached the ship and continued to be besieged by echoes from the shore. Things I'd seen but hadn't particularly noticed—or so I fancied—persisted in pestering me. I lunched in a state of dream, lay down in my cabin, dozed a little and uneasily, opened my eyes:

'There sparkled a fountain, glittered a tank;
The shadows of leaves danced over the wall. . . .

That had been found in Madeira. Glancing in my notebook I found the thing well on the way to completion. The impulse seemed unusually strong. Maybe it would keep further intimations off. For if I went ashore again that day, obviously there'd be more trouble. And yet it was a shame to leave all these beings, animate and inanimate, clamouring. 'It's not exactly what you might call plain murder, but if you leave a poem to die. . .' 'Many are called and few chosen,' I was forced to answer, 'and really, you know, the choice has precious little to do with me—one does what one can. . . .'

After doing what I could, worn out, I had dropped asleep, and here I was awake again. She had anchored. Anchored where? What surrounded her? *New seas, new shores. The feeling of 'arrival.' What does that mean when seas and shores are new?* Hell! Another poem starting; but it didn't feel as if there were much to it. Or if there was, the poem was one of these tenuous affairs that you have to wait for at the intensest stretch. I decided to let it go. Tired. Much too tired. '*New seas, New shores.*' Diminuendo. Words at the other end of a long tunnel. In a moment I shall be asleep . . .

Sometimes I involuntarily all-but-surfaced from the dark sweet depths of my slumber. I knew this happened because phrases in faint rhythm began to turn over in my head with the insistence of a litter of mechanical toys in action. Then down I went again.

Finally I emerged in one steady and triumphant motion. My head went round; the white cabin assembled itself. At once I knew that further sleep was out of the question, that my business was to go on deck, if possible up into the bows by the anchor chains. Wasn't that, I told myself, the obvious thing to do on so glorious a morning? Oh, I was very hearty indeed, very buoyant! But all the time a tiny voice within was saying: 'You're in fine fettle, so refreshed, that undoubtedly a poem will be waiting for you. By and large I'd say that it will probably be about the rising sun.' 'Now look here,' I replied, 'can't you let a fellow alone awhile? I'm hearty, but not as hearty as all that. In any case my heartiness is purely physical. Psychically I'm extremely fatigued. I just want to go up in the bows there and fill my lungs and get completely solid and human again. Fact is,—I'd like to take the whole morning off. At any rate, till well after breakfast. I shall, I assure you, feel very different and more able to cope with things when I've swallowed a good plateful of bacon and eggs. But I can't get that before half-past seven at earliest. And I am so enjoying myself now. Be a good soul and let me bide. Can't you see I'll work much better—if that's what you're after—if only I can have a little rest, if only you will permit my mind to become completely distangled from the phantasmal? Look, for instance, at the beautiful, rich, white, creamy paint in this cabin—every moment I have of it does me good. Can't you understand I like it so much I could lick the stuff off the walls as if it were the cream it resembles? And the heavy brass of the porthole ring and couplings and the brown mahogany of the bunk—how soft, smooth, assuring, satisfactory all that is! These are solid goods; let me enjoy them. I have a dreadful need of solids! Can't you understand that for the moment mere physical being on the lowest animal plane is quite enough for me, that if only you'd leave me alone, I'd roll up in that blanket again and taste the animal pleasure of a renewed and profound sleep? *That* I know is impossible; but have a heart, leave me alone for a little, and let me stroll in my silk dressing gown and pyjamas like a normal passenger enjoying an early cigarette! 'You're awake long before the others,' the voice replied sardonically, 'but enjoy the illusion of liberty if you will and can. Remember however that the sun will soon be highest above the horizon and that, once it is, the light will be of quite a different quality. Get out there as soon as you can. But don't rush. This calm of animal pleasure is useful to you.'

I took my time. Nonetheless within two minutes I was clambering up the iron stairs onto the fo'c'sle.

The ship was miraculously deserted. Upon the spick-and-span bridge the head of the officer of the watch could be descried behind the canvas. He lifted a hand and nodded me good morning.

It appeared we were once more on the move but so slowly that I shouldn't have known it had I not glanced over the side and observed the anchor snugged home and a noiseless ripple stealing about the stem. Yes, we were moving. But no air came over the bows and I was in effect merely standing on a slowly swaying platform amid an immense liquid plain with, as I gazed aft, what looked like a long low cloud on my left: the shore of the Grand Canary. There was no smoke above our funnels, though the air quivered for a hand's breadth over them. This day's life on earth hadn't yet begun.

I shoved my hands into the pockets of my silk dressing-gown —the notebook was there in the right-hand pocket—and drank in the superb chill blandness of the morning air. I was very well satisfied with existence. I felt extremely normal save for an unusual hollowness in my stomach where an unfortunate captive stirred, dreaming of bacon and eggs.

I stared for'ard. Not a sail. Nothing but the enormous tranquil, softly-heaving plain of the sea. Complete silence reigned, one of the most perfect I had ever known. And, what was better yet, there was silence within. I was merely 'being.' Very pleasant, very pleasant indeed! I turned about and lit a cigarette.

The sun had just risen. It was a hot agate-red but not so bright that one couldn't look at it. Some amiable and easy-going artist had diluted brown ink with much water and lightly drawn a full paint-brush round the half circle of the sea's horizon. That is how I describe the scene to myself now. Then I simply looked at it, feeling the delicious buoyancy of the deck beneath my feet and blissfully exhaling a cloud of Turkish tobacco smoke. After a few puffs my cigarette went overboard. There was more pleasure in inhaling the pure air, fresh and delicious as a water-ice.

At that moment the newly-risen sun sent flickering over the long, low, smooth, glassy mounds of the rolling swells a series of elastic reflections which expanded and contracted and zig-zagged and appeared and disappeared and reformed as they travelled in stately and regular motion toward me. . . . .

I became aware of an extraordinary physical exhilaration. 'Of course!' I said to myself—'Arabic.'

It was at that moment, as I now discern, that I understood I had only to yield to the emotion evoked by what I beheld to discover a poem, the potentiality of which existed not only in the characters propelled toward me but all around me, in the entire sea and sky and, more remotely, in my own solitude which, however, wasn't my unique loneliness as it had existed up to that moment—the loneliness of Robert Nichols standing on an iron fo'c'sle—but the solitude of any figure beholding the miracle (and in a state to receive it as such) at any period in history. As I realised this, the hieroglyphics upon the waters seemed to flash through me, that is to say, to pass through my body without occasioning any pain. They continued to do this. My eye dwelled upon the scene and the longer it dwelled—though but a moment passed—the more I was filled with an immense and pure emotion *which was the reflection of what I saw*, that is to say I was conscious of a regular and growing central excitement surrounded by an area of deep, tranquil and joyful satisfaction. This was, I felt, as it should be—I was being told something. Now the existence of this satisfaction, being simply due to the glory of the morning, might have merely remained a state of being for the expression of which words were neither sought nor found, because not felt to be needed, had not the character of the hieroglyphics given a special quality to the emotion possessing me. That change may roughly be defined as a change from the animal to the spiritual. And when I ask myself why that change was affected, I can only reply that the answer lies in the fact that the reflections travelling toward me had the changing shapes that were theirs. Had the reflections been merely blobs of light, had they been written in a script with which I was acquainted, had they for instance formed a succession of capital letters—such as R K P followed by L Z O followed by N Q T—they would, I fancy, have added little, if indeed anything, to my animal pleasure. But they were recognisable, though not decipherable, as units having the peculiarities of a cursive script, rightly or wrongly taken by me to be Arabic and Arabic, I instantly grasped, of a peculiar kind,—golden letters in a holy book, such a book as I knew I had once seen, a book with wooden covers, dated, so I was given to understand, about 1500.* And as these units were so taken—that is to say as golden and written in a holy book (simply that and nothing more)—so I at the same or nearly the same instant apprehended that these figures *weren't* in a book but were, at that very moment, in the most literal sense *being written on the sea by the sun*, a being who was a poet. *I did not say to myself 'the sun is a poet' but I felt the emotion*

---

* Association has up to date failed to give me particulars of when and where.

*such a person as myself might be expected to feel were he to
find himself in the presence of a being both capable of doing
what I now beheld being done and accustomed to doing it.*
There was then a fractional pause, a halt in my attention as
if that attention didn't wholly apprehend what was presented
to it, the halt in fact that precedes recognition. And just as
the memory of a name, for which a face, clothes and person
already exist, brings with it the memory of the circumstances
in which this person was earlier met and many of his or her
attributes and the ideas and atmosphere of like or dislike connected with him or her—what I may call the *myth* of this person
—so on an instant there was presented to my consciousness a
favourite picture-postcard I had twice or thrice bought at the
British Museum. Almost simultaneously there formed in my
mouth the line

'The sun an ancient, serene poet.'

The picture on the postcard—that of a poet, possibly Persian,
seated on the ground, wearing a rose-pink turban, a green
caftan and a little pair of black slippers, and gazing to the
spectator's left—and the line were indissoluble. They remain
indissoluble to this day—in the sense that I cannot repeat the
first line of the poem without seeing the picture on the postcard.
(But should I see the postcard I do not automatically remember
the line. The reader of the poem, of course, never sees the
postcard and has no notion till after the first line that the 'poet'
may not be a European save in so far as the two adjectives
'ancient' and 'serene' used together may suggest an oriental
quality.)
    Did the postcard precipitate the line or the line the postcard?
Neither. The emotion of being in the presence of an august
personage engaged, as I beheld him engaged, precipitated both
the line and the image, an image, which, beautiful though it was,
was felt to be a makeshift, a 'convenient fiction.' For though
the image was emotionally more or less exact—that is to say,
tranquil and suggestive of composed satisfaction—it had two
faults: it was felt both as inadequate to express the force of the
visual experience and in some manner not quite visually correct.
Wherein the incorrectness lay, we shall see in a moment. The
nature of the incorrectness wasn't, of course, analysed at the
time.
    Nevertheless, no sooner was the line created, than I experienced
a feeling of considerable satisfaction, first because there was
as-it-were plenty of time (this being the first line) to supply that
which would by elaboration give what had been stated adequacy
and, second, because there seemed to me something very inclusive
about the line's simplicity (that's to say, it promised well).
I therefore repeated it to myself twice or thrice, partly for its

own sake and partly because I was waiting for what would arrive next—obviously a verb of some sort.

As I repeated the line the personage I call the artificer in the poet drew my attention to the fact that the line

'The sun an ancient, serene poet

was lacking in the serenity it sought, among other things, to convey. It was too 'jumpy.' 'Try shifting the order of the adjectives,' said the artificer, 'and inserting a conjunction between them. That ought to do it. Look—

'The sun a serene and ancient poet.'

No sooner had this change been effected than I recognised that the line had *set* in an order that no subsequent occurrence must be suffered to disturb. (When a line is once really right its rightness is of so sacrosanct a nature that rather than change it the poet—this poet at any rate—will abandon the entire piece. The laws of psychological necessity within the art are absolutely inflexible and the poet's personal integrity is involved in his recognition of and reverence for the fact that a line is right and that nothing in heaven or earth can make it otherwise. If it is changed it may be right for some poem or other, but that poem will not be the poem originally intended.)

I repeated the line with a sort of sober pride and experienced in so doing a revival and magnification of the emotion that had occasioned the line's existence. This magnification was due to the grandeur now in process of being experienced and recognised as nothing less than the essential peculiarity of the scene about me. For the sun was rapidly mounting, the sea becoming brighter and all the effects at once broader and less definite. . . .

The words were beginning to work, the medium to 'step up' the emotion. For what has been already created knows better than the poet what the poem is about. Why, for instance, did the word 'ancient' repeat itself in my mouth with quite such grandeur? Because, as I see it now, the poem wished to call my attention to the fact that it was in this word that I'd find the answer to the riddle of the next step in the poem's development. The poem didn't say 'think about "ancient,"' but 'ancient' as part of the poem was, when I repeated the line, particularly enjoyed and the quality of 'ancientness' was felt as august, mysterious and full of power. I have said I was persuaded—the artificer was probably responsible for this—that the poem must continue with a verb. The grandeur of the feeling induced by appreciating the word 'ancient' assured me that this verb, the first word of the next line, would be of an emphatic nature. I was not surprised, then, to find it what it was when it arrived, bringing with it the rest of the line:

'Stoops and writes on the sunrise sea.'

Looking back, I now quite clearly perceive how this word 'stoops' established itself and why its authority was so extraordinarily complete. And since the proceedings were thoroughly typical of the mysterious logic that obtains in the act of poetical creation I think I should enlarge a little on 'stoops.' The sun was now a handsbreadth above the sea. This implied that in order to write upon the sea, the sun would have to bend forward and downward. So, too, the Persian poet on the postcard, who, however, could only bend toward the left. None of this was, of course, reasoned out. What was apprehended was first, that the physical sun was escaping upward and would have to be brought to correct action at once before it was too late—for once he was really up, the whole poem would be dispersed into nothingness and prove unwriteable—and, second, that a stiffness in the back—after all he was on a postcard!—was native to the Persian, who therefore could not bend, or at least could not bend as was needed. Instinct had apprehended all this and, apprehending it, had bidden me enjoy myself and stimulate myself with the word 'ancient' to the full. Why? Because 'ancient' is not only one of Blake's especial words— that is to say one carrying particularly powerful charge of emotion,—but one of Blake's images. And just as the bearded Persian poet is to be found on a postcard in the British Museum, so Blake's bearded ancient—the Ancient of Days—is to be found on a postcard at the Tate Gallery. That postcard appeared before my eyes and was not separable from the word 'stoops' which arrived in my mouth at the same moment. As was bound of course to be the case, for Blake's figure on the Tate Gallery postcard *stoops* forward and downward directly opposite the spectator (as the sun was opposite me) to divide the waters, and it was the emotion evoked by the instinctive substitution of Blake's figure for the sun my physical eye beheld that set the word 'stoops' upon my lips. Such a substitution has nothing voluntary about it. Here it was the result of the word 'ancient,' a word which, applicable to the Persian, owed its appearance in the poem to the feelings invoked in me by my surroundings, that is to say, feelings of splendour, grandeur and enduringness. To which as a factor of 'involuntariness' should undoubtedly be added the fact that the image of the Persian poet and Blake's image both exist on postcards, copies of both of which I had at one time or another possessed.

I had now, I perceived, the general framework of a* 'situation' and it was with a sense of tingling excitement that I turned to the artificer to find him smilingly confident that not only would the next line make its appearance with the utmost ease but that we should immediately enjoy it. 'I shan't have to do a thing;'

---

* In the Goethean sense, 'Lively feeling of situation, and power to express them, make the poet' (To Eckermann, June 11th, 1825).

he chirruped, 'it's one of these cases which, though they look like descriptions of things, are really transcriptions of experience. For the up-and-downess feeling will give it you' We were not disappointed, for even as the line curtsied its way through my mind

'In softly undulant cyphers of gold

he nudged me, calling my attention to the softness of its motion while I remarked to him 'We shall have the core of the poem entire in a moment.' And sure enough we did. For no sooner had I recognised that all this while—that is since first I had observed the singular nature of the script flickering upon the swell —I had been waiting for the word 'Arabian' (to be placed, the artificer murmured, in such a position as to extract its full musical and evocative value) than the third line ran out into the fourth:

'In softly undulant cyphers of gold
Words of Arabian charactery

Here the artificer rubbed his hands and said 'Listen to those open *a*'s associated with *r*. If that isn't nice to say, what is?'

I had arrived thus far in the poem without having in any rational sense any notion at all what the poem was about. On such occasions the poet doesn't trouble to make any enquiry what the general sense may be, provided he has the feeling that he possesses a *motif*.* Curiosity as to what the 'sense' may be is, in fact, only one of the lesser factors that prompts him to proceed; the chief is desire to allay the feelings he has by 'realising' (as a painter would say) the *motif*. Again this curiosity as to the 'sense' doesn't imply that he for a moment thinks of trying to reduce that sense to what one might call 'a summary matter-of-fact statement'—for in point of fact such a reduction would—were it possible—only 'put him off his stroke,' since it could but be a statement stripped of potency and suggestion, that is to say without emotive quality. Attempt at such reduction can only result in the poet killing what he loves, namely the goose that lays the golden eggs, a goose (be it noted) that must be loved for its own sweet sake. Nevertheless, there comes a time when a certain anxiety makes itself felt. This is of a so-to-speak purely—or mostly—practical kind and has to do with the appropriate development of procedure from the situation already created by the lines in existence. Have the foundational premises been established? If so, are they quite complete? Is the topography of the scene correct? What again of structure—for instance, further arrangement of rhymes, if rhymes are being used? What of—for this sometimes arises—syntax (the most formidable of all niggers in the poetical woodpile)?

* This is where the *gestalt* psychologist spies a whole new territory to make his own. The results may be of a revolutionary importance.

In this case the premises seemed firmly established, that's to say that the necessary visible data reported themselves as seemingly 'all present and correct.' As to rhyme, I cannot remember considering how this poem was going to rhyme. It was felt as a 'free' poem—that is to say one without a pre-ordained definite rhyme-scheme. If I am asked *how* I felt that, I can only answer that I felt it in *my elbows*. I had a literal sense of space, and this sense of space corresponded in some sort to my consciousness of the immense spaces of softly undulating ocean and depth of sky that environed me. As to structure, my instinct was 'This gets bigger, this "snowballs" as it rolls forward to some broad culmination,' a fact that I reported to the artificer.

I now felt myself vaguely threatened by that predicament in which the poet, finding himself in possession of the *motif* in mythic form—or feeling himself well on the way to possessing some substantial portion of it—asks himself 'Well, now, being in this possession, what are we going to do with it?' This is the sort of question which should not be encouraged since it tokens a want of confidence, the mere utterance of which tends to increase any want of confidence that may already exist. Moreover, such a question by introducing the poet's personal volition invites him to indulge in guesswork, to fancy and to run this or that horse. But poetry is knowledge, not guessing. If any question is to be put—and the rarer the question the better— the question should read not 'what do *I* do now?' but 'what is *it* going to do?' Nonetheless, some sort of action has frequently to be taken for fear the poem settle down contentedly on its base and 'stay put.'* The already existent substance has to be both excited and given a little push—that is to say, the lines have to be repeated by the poet in such a manner that they give off some of the emotion they contain and at the same time the rhythm needs to be a little exaggerated in repetition—which happens easily enough if the poem becomes excited—in order that the élan so released may launch the poetic faculty into what comes next or may at least suggest the sort of pulse on which the next line will form.

On this occasion the poem easily became excited. But the trouble was that the emotional flow inherent in the arabesque of the rhythm died away—as, of course, the sense dictated it should—with the full stop at the end of the line. (The artificer has more than once suggested that this full stop should be changed to three dots). A statement on a musical basis, ana-logous to the sense, had been made. Since that statement (so far as it went) was complete a new musical basis would be re-quired when the sense should have picked up again.

* There is a factor of inertia which has to be taken into account when the poet is in 'the musical mood.' Here the action of the conscious is sometimes necessary.

Obviously a sort of inclusive 'pick up' would have to be made.
Meanwhile the tolling of the word 'gold' (at the end of line
three) continued in the inner ear and demanded satisfaction.
For that is what rhymes do, and it is sometimes a very nice
question how much of the poet's attention should be given to
the tone of this demand. An old-hand-at-the-game recognises
almost automatically whether the word is of the sort that as a
rhyme is likely to 'make trouble.' For there are some words
that are very difficult to rhyme to and one at least (silver) for
which no rhyme exists. Usually, however, when the poem is
going nicely and the writer an old hand a lightning glance of
interrogation directed toward the artificer suffices to assure the
old hand that all is well should doubt have arisen. That doubt
is, provided the word doesn't immediately attract attention to
itself (in the sense of being involuntarily recognised as a
'twister'), little likely to arise when the emotion inherent in
what has preceded is strong. Here, as on the battle-field,
morale is of the first importance. There exist indeed some
striking analogies between command in the field and poetical
composition. In both cases lightning decisions have to be taken
in order to meet a rapidly changing situation which is but partly
comprehended and in each case tactical instinct is the chief
instrument of decision. Suffice to say that on this occasion
I heard the syllable 'gold' tolling at the same time that I was
aware that a 'pick-up' was needed. A sense of discomfort
ensued and my 'tactical instinct' instructed me to 'surface'
from the reverie within the poem (that is my constructional
activity among words) to the reverie of the fo'c'sle (that is to
what, for want of a better term, I must call my spiritual life on
the fo'c'sle). In point of fact I went even further and precipitated myself for a moment out of the world wherein poetry
is composed into the world of conscious everyday apprehension
—the world in which one can, if one wishes, count first the davits
along the ship's side, then the stanchions on the bridge, add the
two together, divide the sum by three and multiply the result
by seven, a feat impossible to perform—or which I at least could
not perform—when in 'the reverie of the poem,' or in 'the
reverie of the fo'c'sle' since adding, dividing and so forth have
never become for me, despite school drill, in any sort automatic
activities, but have always demanded and continue to demand
a direct and highly self-conscious concentration of the faculties.*

Such a 'surfacing' into what is by contrast with the world
just left a purely *prose* world—a world apprehended without
much regard to any conscious delight in quality—is always
perilous. For once the poet has returned to it, he may discover

---

* To my thinking the book-keeping and poetical casts of mind are
antithetical. Psychologists might fruitfully investigate the qualities of
memory characteristic of each.

the invisible door, by which return was made, to have been silently closed behind him and find himself stranded in a universe wherein such beauty as may exist, is like to be *perceived* as existent as a quality of the scene but not *felt* as such. Permanent sojourn in such a universe, without prospect of escaping this apotheosis of the Meaningless, is hell. Hell has indeed for the poet no other connotation.*

Why then did I 'surface'—a simple process, consisting of shaking myself as a man may do to abolish drowsiness—into a so (comparatively speaking) inhospitable world? *First*, I wanted a moment's relaxation and felt the spiritual life so strong in me that I had no doubt of being able to return to it the very instant I desired so to do, provided my 'spy-hop' was minimal, and, *second*, as I have said, tactical instinct, prompted (I fancy) by the artificer, instructed me to do so. This prompting might be said to amount to a smile from the artificer signifying 'Pretty good, guv'nor, but there's something in these 'ere arrangements which ain't quite ship-shape. They're all right so far as they go, but they don't go far enough. Put up your nose—no harm in coming up for air a moment—while "gold" stays tolling. That tolling will keep things together here below, while you're gone,—provided, of course, you return as soon as possible.' That's, of course, how I read his smile now. At the time it was merely a smile, such a smile being usually sufficient to imply all that's needed. (The less noise in the workshop the better.)

I emerged on deck without difficulty.† The morning heat was already sufficient for me to notice the warmth of the metal plates beneath the soles of my thin slippers, to cause me to remark the crawling iridescence of the particles that composed the black paint upon that metal, and for me to smell the faint coaldusty odour of the air rising from those plates. On the bridge the officer of the watch had shifted not his position but his attitude, and was leaning his elbows upon the canvas. He had shoved his cap on to the back of his head and was scratching the hair above his ear. The tremor of the air over the funnels was more pronounced and its wanderings were more fluid. All around shone the expanse of the immense and rapidly whitening sea with, on my left, the island, now more of an island and less of a cloud, and, forward on my right, the disc of the sun still rolling characters of glittering liquidity toward me. So much brighter, broader and more irregular indeed had the glitter of those characters become that what I now beheld less and less resembled definite characters and more and more resolved itself

---

* Hence the undoubted antipathy between some poetical minds and the lowlier type of scientific worker, the paradise of the second being the inferno of the first.

† This is not always easy to effect by volition in cases when the work is to be continued almost immediately.

into a series of burning flashes. And it was evident that soon I should no longer see separate flashes flickering from undulation to undulation but a burnished and continuous path.

Meanwhile I was conscious that what I saw amounted to a statement of *isolation*: I stood on a moving ship and the shore hung stationary several miles away. No sooner had I gathered this information—and gathered it in a thoroughly matter of fact way—than I sank back into the workshop beside the artificer. The word 'gold' was still tolling—it had never ceased to toll while I was on deck—and I whispered to him 'Look here—this is the trouble: I am on a ship and our viewer-of-the-sunrise is obviously upon the shore. You're right, we haven't quite completed the arrangements necessary before we can proceed and make our "pick up." We haven't all the "situation," for our topography isn't complete.'

The artificer tactfully disappeared (he knows his job) and I inspected, coldly enough, the memory I had brought from my visit to the deck. Obviously our viewer was standing on a beach, a beach such as might exist yonder on the island. The wet pebbles would be glittering. . .

I detected a sense of effort. I was 'imagining.' I was 'making things up.' I relaxed, sought the association of the glittering pebbles and found myself standing, as so often in past summers, upon Winchelsea beach. The sultry, lustreless sea, perfectly calm and as though half-stupefied by the heat, was rolling a few pebbles up and down the pebble-bank in a listless and perfunctory manner. . .

So there the rhyme was: 'rolled.'

Having discovered this, I perceived that the words which would follow 'rolled' would give me the position of our viewer. This satisfied me that our topography was now sufficiently complete in a provisional sense ('gold' had ceased tolling) to allow me to return to my poem.

I read my lines over:

> 'The sun, a serene and ancient poet,
> Stoops and writes on the sunrise sea
> In softly undulant cyphers of gold
> Words of Arabian charactery.'

Serenity and happiness possessed me and I felt the ship's slight and easy rocking. I read the lines again more slowly and perceived that it was the motion of the ship that had yielded them the rhythm they had. For I yielded to that motion and was cradled into the reverie of my spiritual life upon the deck. I lifted my eyes with reverence to the scene and no longer felt isolation. Love filled the empyrean.

I returned to the workshop:

> 'And the riddle is lovingly rolled'

'All very well, but that water isn't lolling,' interjected the artificer. Try
> 'And the lovely riddle is lovingly rolled

'Isn't that a little affected?' I asked.

'I think it's all right,' he said, 'you want to *dwell*, don't you?'

'Yes,' I said:
> 'And the lovely riddle is lovingly rolled
> Toward my feet. What is here enscrolled?'

'For that's how it goes on, I'm sure. "What is here enscrolled" is our "pick up." It must be. Haven't we said the charactery is a "riddle"? Isn't that what we've felt from the first? Isn't mystery what we're after?'

'Yes,' he said, 'but there's something missing. You do the feeling and I'll do the hearing, which is after all only the echo of your feeling. I think, mind you, I shall have to be a bit "clever" here. But "cleverness" is legitimate if it "comes off."'

We remained silent and I descended into a deep drowse in which I could no longer—as I had no wish to—distinguish the slight roll of the ship from the welling of the water up and down Winchelsea beach. I became immersed in one of those long afternoons at the close of which one feels, rather than hears, afar off the reverberations of thunder, a reverberation hardly distinguishable from the rolling of a weight of pebbles up and down a long curve of beach. . . .
> 'With sound of slumberous peaceful thunder'—

'Is that it, artificer? Do you hear it?'

'Certainly I do. And very nice too. It helps to *place* our viewer in the sense of giving him *isolation*.'

'Listen,' I said, 'there is love everywhere, and there is also a sort of loneliness. Listen hard and you'll hear the love that is in the sky *talking* out of its loneliness to the loneliness on the beach.'

'Is it "*in*" the sky?' he said.

'No,' I said, 'it's around the sky.'

'Well, then,' he said, 'why not say so? "Around the sky." "Around the sky" gives you not only space and stillness and distance but sound, the echo of the "sound" of the "slumberous, peaceful thunder." After which, of course, we've got to bring it back to "Toward my feet" and that implies mention of the sea. There's something in Tennyson, though I can't recollect exactly what. In *The Vision of Sin* perhaps. Did you hear any echo to the thunder just now?'

'Yes,' I said, 'but, I was waiting for you. It seemed so slight that I didn't know whether it was catchable.'

'We've got to believe everything's catchable. As a matter of fact, I did have an idea, but it seemed to me a trifle too professional, too slick.'

'Yes?'

'So I didn't offer it.   D'you want it?'

'No harm in looking at it.'

'There's the word "thereunder."'

'Perfect!' I said, 'of course.   It isn't only structurally right—in that it gives the rhyme—it is useful in assisting the evocation of the scene.   For it gives the flatness of the sea under the half-dome of the sky and the semi-circle of the sea's rim.'

We stood back and examined the affair:

> 'And the lovely riddle is lovingly rolled
> With sound of slumberous, peaceful thunder
> Around the sea and the sky thereunder
> Toward my feet.

'Must we have that ".toward my feet?"'

'Got to.'   I said.   'Maybe we can carry it.'

The artificer repeated the lines voluptuously, mouthing the vowels and labials.   'My!' he said, 'I don't often get such an innings.   That's art, that is.   You can't tell it from inspiration except for that word "lovely."   I don't like that and I never shall, but I guess it's got to stand.   For the rest, the passage is pretty artful.'

'Yes,' I said, 'it's art; but you couldn't have got it except for my drowse.'

'Of course,' he said hastily, 'of course; all the same it's a dandy bit of psychological engineering, though I say it as shouldn't—being largely responsible.   Wonderful the properties in the sounds of words—if you know how to place 'em and how to exploit their properties.'

The artificer, I may remark, is, though enthusiastic, a lazy fellow. Any excuse for a chat.   He has all the presumption of a *famulus* who, alas, knows he's indispensable.   He has, too, a certain insensibility and is without moods.   Perhaps he can't afford to have moods—after all I do keep him hanging about in the most outrageous fashion once we're on the job.   And I'm bound to say, first, that he'll tackle anything, if put to it, at any hour of the day or night and, second, that once actually at work, he's exceedingly painstaking.   What I like best about him is that his professional conscience can't be squared in any manner whatsoever (he protests to this day against the retention of that word 'lovely').   Against which I must set the fact that he is extravagantly vain, has no formal reverence for me whatsoever (though he 'knows his place') and is very impatient with anybody who presumes to criticise his handiwork.   He is, I may add, entirely self-taught, harbours plausible theories on which he is inclined to be garrulous, and doesn't (any more than I do) know a dactyl from a spondee.   Though his method is empirical, he seems to know the unusable at sight.   His opinions on the public are quite unprintable.   To listen to him you'd think there weren't in these islands more than a dozen persons—if that—capable of understanding the machinery of poetry. His contempt is blasting. I'm a little bit afraid of him (he's somewhat of a puritan). He regards me with tolerant affection as a remarkable being and, in my way, a fellow professional: in fact his attitude toward me resembles that of a first class laboratory assistant toward a mysterious, absent-minded, but undoubtedly able old professor. 'Nobody,' I've heard him declare (he likes a chat with others of his ilk) 'nobody knows what goes on in the guv'nor's head—I don't believe he knows himself—but on his day he's a winner, he is.'

'*Toward my feet. What is here enscrolled?*' murmured the artificer. And then suddenly in that jaunty manner he sometimes assumes and which I particularly detest, 'And what precisely, guv'nor, on the square, *entre nous* and in strict confidence is enscrolled? I mean I've got to make my arrangements.'

'I haven't the slightest idea,' I returned coolly.

'You seem pretty confident!'

'I am'; I replied, 'time to worry when we come to the moment in which we ought to know and find we don't. As a matter of fact, we shan't worry. What's enscrolled is writ very large, and I know it is to be read at the end of the poem. For that is what the entire poem leads to.'

'But I want to know about it now,' he persisted. 'Honest, guv'nor—no *blague*—I must. There's rhymes and all sorts of things to keep an eye open for. Moreover, there's the movement. If we're going to open up in a big way for our close—'

'And we are. That's what it feels like.'

'We've got to *roll* toward it, haven't we? I mean it's got to "snowball." Remember I can't go outside—can't go further than the open doorway. And that's not near enough to see to the end of the poem. It follows that I can't make a workmanlike job of this affair unless I have some idea of our whitherward, even if the sense of the whitherward is not conveyed in words at all but is only a sort of pulse and an indication of the quantity of sound-volume likely to be required.'

'Well,' I said, 'the stuff snowballs and returns on itself and piles itself up and at last the secret of it all comes out *fortissimo* (on the trombones, so to speak). Everything coupled up. Grand organ effect.'

'Okay, guv'nor, okay; I get you. But to get the proper sort of lead up to the climax I've got to *have* that climax whatever it is. Two last lines I suppose it'll be, giving me two rhymes to play with on my climb. Come, guv'nor, is it two lines? I simply gotta know. Don't lose your nerve.'

(He is confoundedly perspicacious. I was, in point of fact, becoming distinctly nervous. Well pleased with the opening of my poem, I trembled to think of so promising an affair coming to nought.)

'Take a turn,' he said, 'try the old dodge: forget you're writing a poem at all. And you needn't worry about the rhyme. We've nothing here save the "gold" rhyme (if you need it), nothing, I mean, obligatory. There's a lot to come between what we have and the last two lines. So go ahead. We're out for something big. I feel just as enthusiastic about this poem as you do. So don't worry about the rhymes on the end of those last two lines. I'll fix 'em somehow!'

I thrust my notebook into my pocket and took a turn or two The characters had almost entirely disappeared from the sea's surface. Light, peace, purity and splendour surrounded me. All was so beautiful that at that moment I no longer cared whether I finished my poem or not: enough to exist between that perfect sky and sea and feel their perfection!

I pulled out my notebook and scribbled hastily:

> 'The Heavens declare the glory of God
> And the Firmament showeth his Handiwork.'

I hadn't the faintest idea where this had come from or any doubt whatever but that this was the conclusion and had been intended as such from the first.

I handed it to the artificer.

'Pretty neat,' he said, 'pretty neat. But you've been and gone and done just what I was afraid you would. I had a notion that word "God" was about—the content seemed to point to the likelihood of it turning up. And "God"—it's the deuce of a word to rhyme to! Don't you know that by this time, guv'nor? You know how it goes—"hod," "nod," "shod," "odd," "plod," and so forth: not many rhymes and mostly awkward! "Period" makes a bit of a change. But, whatever it is, the rhyme to "God" nearly always looks what it usually is—dragged in.'

'I'm sorry,' I said, 'but there's no option. We'll have to do what we can.'

'And "handiwork,"' he proceeded. '"Handiwork"! You've certainly set us a pretty problem this time and no mistake with your "god" and "handiwork".'

'What about Turk?' I said lightly, 'ever heard of "Greek," Jew, Infidel and Turk"?'

'You're joking'; he said, 'surely you can't mean that?'

'Well, "handiwork" ends our last line and we've got to rhyme to it. Stranger things have happened.'

'Noted, guv'nor, noted. But I wish I shared your good spirits. Strikes me there's going to be a lot of—what d'you call it?—"artifact" about our penultimate line.'

'Well,' I answered, 'we've got a strong current of feeling and

that tends to keep things alive, however "artifact" they may be. Where were we?'
   'Toward my feet. What is here enscrolled?'
 'Well, we know now what is. Let's look at it. "The Heavens declare the glory of God"; that's a poem. "Handiwork seems to imply history. I have it:
   'Is it a poem or a story?'
 'And afterwards you reverse it,' the artificer interjected. 'And, if I might suggest something, guv'nor . . . there's that word "charactery"—that's a nice word. Nice enough in fact to use twice if need be. Gives you an easy rhyme, too. And we need stuff we can play about with hereabouts because we'll be in for difficult going later on. Nothing like having an easy rhyme to work with if you're afraid of trouble ahead, especially syntactical trouble.'
 'Don't fuss so;' I said, 'this is going to be all right. I only need a run at it. Give me the notebook. Now I'm going to make my mind a blank and run through the stuff we've got. For, if it gets excited, I fancy we'll be able to go ahead without undue trouble.'
 I ran through all we had and found I wasn't mistaken. It continued of itself—
   . . . . . . 'What is here enscrolled?
   Is it a poem or a story?
   I cannot command this charactery.'
By this time the poem was thoroughly excited and I myself uplifted.
 'Round *o*'s, round *o*'s!' cried the artificer. 'Belt 'em in! Belt 'em in! One big one right away! And then as many as you can manage.'
   'But I think it is bOth and that it reads
   This glOrious mOrning as of Old—'
The poem became very excited indeed. I went to the ship's side and swept the horizon with my eye. 'By Jove,' I said, 'yes!—of course!
   'When the first sun rose above the first sea'—
I say, artificer, think of that!—"*When the first sun rose above the first sea.*" What a picture!'
 'Nice, guv'nor, nice. But don't stop to admire it or you may lose something. Continue. Keep it moving. Hold that tone, keep it grand, keep it tense. I've a rhyme handy you've forgotten if you need one.'
 'Yes, we sustain the feeling—
   "As read it will while there is sea
   And sun to scribe with"—
with what?'

'I'm holding "gold" for you, guv'nor.'

"with reed of gold"

'Yes:

"As read it will while there is sea
And sun to scribe with reed of gold."'

'I don't like "reed," guv'nor. You've got the same sound with
a different sense in the line before. Nothing doing. Can't
stand for it.'

'Guess you've got to.'

'What about "quill of gold"?'

'But a Persian poet doesn't write with a quill. He writes,
I fancy, with a sort of reed.'

'Never mind what you fancy, guv'nor. This time it ain't
evidence. I can't stand for "reed," guv'nor; sorry, but I just
can't, we're talking about the sun anyway.'

'Pity—I like the notion of a reed pen. But, after all, there
was a sort of dagger-like brightness running down the centre of
what I saw early on. "Quill"? Yes, it'll have to be "quill."
I don't altogether like it. It will take some getting used to,
but I suppose we've got to have it.'

'And now your "return," guv'nor!' The artificer had become
very energetic indeed. (He gets these fits of what I may call
'muscular' energy. They have, I think, something to do with
the rhythmical side of his job. If we don't keep going in a
situation of this sort the whole affair may 'die on us' or not be
found again for weeks.)

'It doubles back on itself;' he said, 'that's the structure of
it—so doing, it gives us, you see, another run at the rhythm
and helps the snowballing. See, guv'nor?'

I didn't bother to pause to find out whether I saw or no. On
these occasions one gives the fellow his head.

'It is both poem and a story.'

'No! No! Reverse 'em this time; gives variety. See here:—

"It is both story and a poem."

'All right I'll try it. But don't interrupt again—we're getting
to the end of immediate collaboration. I'll have to leave the
workshop in a minute. We can't just hack our way through,
I know that.'

"It is both story and a poem,
A hymn, as also a history"—

'No. Nothing doing. We're getting excited. I'll have to
dream it.'

I returned to the reverie of the deck.

'It is both story and a poem' . . .

I said to myself. 'That's emphatic, that's strophic. There's majesty here. Calm down. It's beginning to broaden. And nothing like broadening for using one up.'

I began to feel tired.

'There is also mystery in it,' I reflected.

I went and leaned against the rail. 'Goethe would know,' I said to myself. 'What a pity one isn't Goethe. Evidently he had no trouble at all. Did this sort of thing almost without knowing he was doing it. But then he was a mage. Well?— of course!—

> 'as also a history
> Concerning the mightiest of mages.'

I was becoming very tired indeed. I wrote that down. The artificer appeared.

'There's that easy rhyme;' he said, 'I've saved it for you. Rhyme to "sea," and, in a lesser sense, "history." Come along, guv'nor, we're nearly in the straight. Lift it up again. Stay up and keep it strophic.'

> 'The best that has been or shall be . . .'

"Ages," "ages," "ages," he said, 'that's a nice rhyme for "mages." Get to that.'

> 'The best that has been or shall be
> Writ for any throughout the ages.

'That what you want?' I said, 'I don't see it.' I said, 'I just don't see it.'

'What about that "Greek, Jew, Infidel and Turk" of yours?' he grinned. 'Written *for* somebody and written *by* somebody. And then there's that word to rhyme with "God." A plodding scholar. Let me work it out for you.'

I seated myself on the bollard. I needed rest.

Presently he returned. 'Nothing doing,' he said, 'but it's there. Just a question of hard work later on. You give me the "join up" for the last two lines and I'll do it when you're fresh and can judge it. I'd like another rhyme to "sea" if you can make it. It would be nice to have a sort of drop before the big announcement. A sort of hush.'

'Yes,' I said absently. 'I know what you mean. There is a penultimate state of feeling, though what Lord alone knows.' He tiptoed away.

> 'For Greek, Jew, Infidel and Turk'—

'Yes,' I thought, 'but why for them only? It is for all of us.' I looked at the hushed sky and sea. 'However perfect it is,' I said to myself, 'I shall never get it. I can only look at it and wonder. . . . Ah, the penultimate state of feeling—humility, of course:

> "As it was written, too, for me."

And then majesty. Something decisive!'

I looked once more on the glory about me.   'The sky and the sea,' I said to myself, 'they are one, and yet they are two'—

> 'One page, two eternal sentences'—

'Yes, that's it'—

> 'One page, two eternal sentences!
> The Heavens declare the glory of God,
> And the Firmament showeth His Handiwork.'

It was done.   I handed it to the artificer, reached my cabin and lay down.   My watch was lying on the counterpane.   I glanced at it.   Twenty minutes had passed.

When I woke it was eleven o'clock and I had missed my bacon and eggs.

Bibliography

NOTE.—In order not to lengthen the Bibliography unduly, extracts or references which occur on two or more consecutive pages in the same chapter are not referred to separately. For example, if an extract occurs on page 41 and another on page 42, the reader is referred in each case to pp. 41–42.

The + against a reference in the Bibliography denotes a quotation in the book.

ALLAN (G.). *Life of Sir Walter Scott.* Edinburgh: Thomas Ireland, jun., 1834.
+(1) p. 326.

ALTMANN (W.). *Letters of Wagner.* Edited by W. Altmann. See WAGNER.

AUBREY (J.). *Minutes of the Life of Mr. John Milton.* Contained in *The Early Lives of Milton.* Edited by H. Darbishire. London: Constable & Co., Ltd. 1932.
+(2) p. 13.

AUSTEN LEIGH (J. E.). *A Memoir of Jane Austen.* 2nd edition. London: Richard Bentley & Son. 1871.
(3) p. 96.
(4) pp. 147–48.

BAIN (Alexander). *The Senses and the Intellect.* 4th edition. London: Longmans, Green & Co. 1894.
+(5) p. 352.

BALFOUR (Graham). *Life of Robert Louis Stevenson.* 2 vols. London: Methuen & Co., Ltd. 1901.
(6) Vol. 1, pp. 99–100.
+(7) Vol. 2, pp. 141–42.

BEETHOVEN. *Impressions of Contemporaries.* London: Oxford University Press. 1927.
+(8) pp. 164–65.
(9) pp. 168–69.

—— *Beethoven's Letters.* 2 vols. Critical edition with notes by Dr. A. C. Kalischer. Translated by J. S. Shedlock. London: J. M. Dent & Sons, Ltd. 1909. By permission also of Messrs. E. P. Dutton & Co., Inc.
+(10) Vol. 1, p. 32, letter No. XXXVI.

BIELSCHOWSKY (Albert). *Life of Goethe.* 3 vols. Translated by W. A. Cooper. New York and London: G. P. Putnam's Sons. 1905, 1907, 1908. (Now Messrs. Putnam & Co., Ltd.)
(11) Vol. 1, p. 189.
+(12) Vol. 3, p. 31.
(13)   „ pp. 38–40.
+(14)   „ p. 69.
+(15)   „ p. 78.
+(16)   „ p. 163.
(17)   „ p. 174.

BIRNSTINGL (E.) and POLLARD (A.). *Corot.* London: Methuen & Co., Ltd. 1904.
(18) p. 95.
(19) pp. 136–37.

BLAKE (William). *The Letters of William Blake* together with a *Life* by William Tatham. Edited from the originxl manuscripts, with introduction and notes, by Archibald G. B. Russell. London: Methuen & Co., Ltd. 1906.

+(20) p. 115 Letter No. 25 to Thomas Butts. 1803.

BLESSINGTON (*Countess* of) *A Journal of the Conversations of Lord Byron with the Countess of Blessington.* New and revised edition. London: R. Bentley & Son. 1893.

+(21) p. 106.
+(22) pp. 119–20.
+(23) p. 330.

BOEHME (Jakob). *The Works of Jacob Behmen* . . . Vol 1, containing I. The Aurora. II. The Three Principles. To which is prefixed The Life of the Author . . . by the Reverend William Law. . . . . London. 1764.

+(24) pp. xiv–xv.

BOULTON (W. B.). *Thomas Gainsborough.* London: Methuen & Co., Ltd. 1905.

+(25) p. 305.
+(26) p. 311.

BUCKLEY (R. J.) *Sir Edward Elgar.* London: John Lane, 1905. Messrs. John Lane: The Bodley Head, Ltd.

+(27) pp. 75–76.

B[URNE]-J[ONES] (G.). *Memorials of Edward Burne-Jones.* 2 vols. London: Macmillan & Co., Ltd. 1904.

(28) Vol. 1, pp. 97–98.
(29)   „   pp. 140–41.

BURNS (Robert). *Letters.* Edited by J. De Lancy Ferguson. 2 vols. Oxford: Clarendon Press. 1931.

+(30) Vol. 2, pp. 194–95, letter 582.
+(31)   „   pp. 200–201, „ 586.

BUSSY (Dorothy). *Eugène Delacroix.* London: Duckworth & Co. 1907. (See also BAUDELAIRE (Charles). *L'Art Romantique*, I, L'Oeuvre et la vie d'Eugène Delacroix.)

+(32) pp. 113–114.

CALVOCORESSI (M. D.) and ABRAHAM (G.). *Masters of Russian Music.* London: Duckworth. 1936.

(33) p. 110.

CAMPBELL (L.) and GARNETT (W.). *The Life of James Clerk Maxwell.* London: Macmillan & Co., Ltd. 1882.

(34) p. 53.
+(35) p. 105.
+(36) pp. 259–60.

CARLYLE (T.). *Life of Friedrich Schiller.* 2nd edition. London: Chapman & Hall. 1845.

(37) p. 108.
(38) pp. 159–60.

CARO (E. M.). *George Sand.* London: George Routledge & Sons. 1888.

+(39) p. 172.
+(39A) p. 129.

CARROLL (Lewis) Art. in *The Theatre.* April 1, 1887 (Vol. IX New Series.).
+(40A) pp. 180–181.

CARTWRIGHT (Julia). *Jean-François Millet.* London: Swan, Sonnenschien & Co. 1902. By permission of Messrs. George Allen & Unwin, Ltd., London.

+(40) p. 347.
+(41) pp. 387–88.

BIBLIOGRAPHY 129

CLAYDEN (P. W.). *The Early Life of Samuel Rogers.* London: Smith, Elder & Co. 1887. By permission of Messrs. John Murray, London.
+(42) pp. 66–67.
CLEMENS (Clara). *My Father: Mark Twain.* New York and London: Harper & Brothers. 1931.
+(43) p. 79.
+(44) p. 208.
+(45) p. 261.
CHARTERIS (*Hon. Sir* Evan). *John Sargent.* London: William Heinemann, Ltd. 1927.
+(46) pp. 71, 77–78.
+(47) p. 158.
COLERIDGE (Samuel Taylor). *Biographia Epistolaris.* 2 vols. Edited by A. Turnbull. London: G. Bell & Sons. 1911.
+(48) Vol. 1, p. 217, letter 99.
+(49)   ,,   ,,   ,, 100.
+(50)   ,, p. 249, letter 109.
        [See also his poem 'A Day Dream':—'My eyes make pictures when they are shut' and his play, *Remorse*, Act ii, Sc. 2:—'His very eyes make pictures of them.']
—— *Biographia Literaria.* 2 vols. Edited by J. Shawcross. Oxford: Clarendon Press. 1907.
+(51) Vol. 2, p. 12.
—— *Letters.* 2 vols. Edited by E. H. Coleridge. London: William Heinemann, Ltd. 1895.
+(52) Vol 1, p. 341, letter CXIII.
—— *Poetical Works.* 2 vols. Edited by E. H. Coleridge. Oxford: Clarendon Press. 1912.
(53) Vol. 1, pp. 295–96.
+(54) Vol. 2, p. 1106 (Appendix III, Preface to 'Fire, Famine and Slaughter,' lines 418–21).
(54A) Vol. 2, p. 1108 (Appendix IV, 'Prose Versions of Poems,' etc.).
—— *Poetical Works.* 2 vols. Edited by T. Ashe. London: George Bell & Sons. 1885.
+(55) Vol. 1, p. 187.
COLVIN (*Sir* Sidney). *John Keats.* London: Macmillan & Co., Ltd. 1920.
(56) p. 143. (Bailey's memoranda of Keat's visit to him at Oxford about 1817.)
+(57) p. 254.
CONRAD (Joseph) *A Personal Record.* London: J. M. Dent & Sons. 1919. By permission of Messrs. B. Pinker & Son (Talbot House, Arundel Street, Strand, London), on behalf of the executors.
+(58) p. 187.
CONRAD (Jessie). *Conrad as I knew him.* London: William Heinemann. 1926.
(59) p. 22.
COOK (*Sir* E. T.) *Life of John Ruskin.* 2 vols. London: George Allen & Co., 1911. Messrs. George Allen & Unwin, Ltd.
+(60) Vol. 1, pp. 126–27. (See Ruskin's *Praeterita*, Vol. XXXV of 'Complete Works' edited by Cook and Wedderburn. London: Allen & Unwin, 1908, p. 311 and pp. 314–15).
COTTLE (Joseph). *Reminiscences of Samuel Taylor Coleridge and Robert Southey.* 2nd edition. London: Houlston & Stoneman. 1848.
+(61) p. 455 (Letter to Thomas Wedgwood).

CROSS (J. W.) *George Eliot's Life as related in her letters and Journals.* 3 vols. Arranged and edited by J. W. Cross. Edinburgh and London: William Blackwood & Sons, Ltd. 1885.

+(63)   „   p. 285 [The story was Silas Marner].
+(64)   „   pp. 313 and 319.
+(65)   Vol. 3, pp. 421–25.

DARBISHIRE (H.). *The Early Lives of John Milton.* Edited by H. Darbishire. London: Constable & Co., Ltd. 1923. See AUBREY, PHILLIPS, TOLAND, RICHARDSON.

DARWIN (C.). *Autobiography.* Thinker's Library, No. 7. London: Watts & Co., 2nd impression. 1931. By permission of Messrs. John Murray.

+(66)   pp. 72–73.
+(67)   p. 75.

DARWIN (*Sir* Francis). *Life and Letters of Charles Darwin.* Edited by his son, Sir Francis Darwin. 3 vols. London: John Murray, 1887.

+(68)   Vol 1, pp. 148–49.

DAUDET (L.). *Alphonse Daudet.* Translated by C. de Kay. London: Sampson Low, Marston & Co. 1898. By permission of the publishers and of *M.* Eugène Fasquelle: Bibliothèque Charpentier, Paris.

+(69)   p. 37.
+(70)   pp. 71–72.
 (71)   p. 82.
+(72)   pp. 84–85.
+(73)   pp. 156–57.

DE LA MARE (Walter). *Behold this Dreamer.* London: Faber and Faber, 1939.

 (73A) p. 97

DICKENS (Charles). *The Letters of Charles Dickens.* Edited by his Sister-in-Law and his eldest Daughter. London: Macmillan & Co., Ltd. 1893.

+(74)   p. 365.
+(75)   p. 377.
+(76)   p. 391.

D'ISRAELI (Isaac). *The Literary Character.* 3rd edition. 2 vols. London. 1822.

+(77)   Vol. 1, pp. 240–41.
+(78)   „   p. 237.
+(79)   Vol. 2, pp. 11–12.

DOSTOEVSKY (Anna Grigorevna, *Mme.* F.). *Dostoevsky portrayed by his Wife.* Translated and edited by S. S. Koteliansky. London: George Routledge & Sons. 1926.

 (80)   p. 152.

DOSTOEVSKY (F. M.). *Letters to his Family and Friends.* Translated by E. C. Mayne. London: Chatto & Windus (and The Macmillan Company of New York). 1914.

+(81)   pp. 100–101.
+(82)   p. 209.
+(83)   p. 257.

DOWNEY (June E.). *Creative Imagination.* 'International Library of Psychology.' Kegan Paul, Trench, Trubner & Co. 1929.

 (84)   p. 167.
 (85)   pp. 192–93.

DUNN (Henry Treffry). *Recollections of Dante Gabriel Rossetti and his circle.*
Edited by Gale Pedrick. London: Elkin Mathews. 1904.
By permission of Gale Pedrick, Esq.
(86) p. 19.
+(87) p. 64.
DURET (Théodore). *Manet and the French Impressionists.* Translated by
J. E. Crawford Flitch. London: Grant Richards, 1910. The
Richards Press, Ltd.
+(88) pp. 139, 142-43.
DYER (F. L.) and MARTIN (T. C.). *Edison, His Life and Inventions.* 2 vols.
New York and London: Harper & Brothers. 1910.
(89) Vol. 1, p. 64.
(90) " p. 278.
+(91) Vol. 2, p. 620.
ELWIN (M.). *Thackeray: A Personality.* London: Jonathan Cape. 1932.
(92) p. 219.
EPSTEIN (Jacob) and HASKELL (A. L.) *The Sculptor Speaks.* London:
William Heinemann, Ltd. 1931.
+(93) p. 115.
FAGUET (E.). *Balzac.* Translated by W. Thorley. London: Constable &
Co. 1918.
(94) p. 31.
FERGUSON (J. de L.). *Letters of Robert Burns.* Edited by J. de L.
Ferguson. 2 vols. Oxford: Clarendon Press. 1931. See
BURNS.
FONTENELLE (B. le B. de). *Life of Sir Isaac Newton with an account of his
writings.* London. 1728.
+(95) p. 24.
FORMAN (M. Buxton). *The Letters of John Keats.* Edited by M. Buxton
Forman. London: Oxford University Press. 1935. See
KEATS.
FORSTER (J.). *Life and Times of Oliver Goldsmith.* 2nd edition. 2 vols.
London: Bradbury & Evans. 1854.
+(96) Vol. 2, pp. 141-42.
—— *Life of Charles Dickens.* Edited by J. W. T. Ley. London: Cecil
Palmer. 1928.
(97) p. 299.
+(98) p. 423.
(99) p. 485, note 313.
(100) p. 720.
—— *Walter Savage Landor.* 2 vols. London: Chapman & Hall, Ltd.
1869.
+(101) Vol. 1, p. 259.
+(102) " p. 269.
FROLOV (Y. P.). *Pavlov and his School.* Translated by C. P. Dutt.
London: Kegan Paul, Trench, Trubner & Co. 1937.
(103) p. 265.
FULLER-MAITLAND (J. A.). *Brahms.* London: Methuen & Co., Ltd. 1911.
+(104) pp. 69-70.
GALT (John). *Life of Lord Byron.* 3rd edition. 'The National Library,
No. 1.' London. 1830.
(105) p. 354.
GALTON (*Sir* Francis). *Enquiries into the Human Faculty and its Development.* 'Everyman Library,' No. 263. London: J. M. Dent
& Sons. 1928. By permission also of Messrs. E. P. Dutton
& Co., Inc.
+(106) p. 146.
—— *Thoughts without words.* Letter in *Nature*, Thursday, 12th May,
1887. London: Macmillan & Co., Ltd.
+(107) p. 29.

GARDNER (Edmund G.). *Saint Catherine of Siena.* London: J. M. Dent & Co. 1907. Messrs. J. M. Dent & Sons, Ltd. By permission also of Messrs. E. P. Dutton & Co., Inc.

+(108) p. 371.

GASKELL (E. C.). *Life of Charlotte Brontë.* Reprinted from the 1st edition. London: Downey & Co. 1901.

+(109) p. 80.
+(110) pp. 283–85.
+(111) p. 364.
 (112) p. 504.
+(113) p. 506.

GILCHRIST (Alexander). *Life of William Blake.* 2 vols. London: Macmillan & Co., Ltd. 1880.

+(114) Vol. 1, p. 364.
+(115)   „   p. 415.

GOGH (Vincent van). *Letters of Vincent van Gogh to his Brother* (1872–86). 2 vols. London: Constable & Co,. Ltd. 1927.

+(116) Vol. 1. From the 'Memoir by his Sister-in-law, p. li.
+(117) p. 526, letter 233.
—— *Further Letters of Vincent van Gogh to his Brother* (1886–89). London: Constable & Co., Ltd. 1929.

+(118) p. 215, letter 546.
+(119) p. 251, letter 561.

GOSSE (Edmund). *Gray.* 'English Men of Letters Series.' London: Macmillan & Co., Ltd. 1882.

 (120) p. 66.
—— *Life of Algernon Charles Swinburne.* London: Macmillan & Co., Ltd. 1917.

 (121) pp. 241–42.

GRAVES (C. L.). *Hubert Parry: His Life and Works.* 2 vols. London: Macmillan & Co., Ltd. 1926.

+(122) Vol. 1, p. 277.
 (123)   „   p. 293.
 (124) Vol. 2, p. 120.
+(125)   „   p. 335 (Extract from his unpublished book 'Instinct and Character').

GRAY (Thomas). *Correspondence of Thomas Gray.* Edited by P. Toynbee and L. Whibley. 3 vols. Oxford: Clarendon Press. 1935.

+(126) Vol. 2, p. 541, letter 257.
+(127)   „   p. 571, „   271.

GROVE (*Sir* George). *Beethoven.* Article in 'Grove's Dictionary of Music.' Vol. 1, 3rd edition. Edited by H. C. Colles. London: Macmillan & Co. 1927.

 (128) p. 272.

GUYON (Madame). *Autobiography of Madame Guyon.* English translation by Thomas Taylor Allen. 2 vols. London: Kegan Paul, Trench, Trubner & Co. 1897.

+(129) Vol. 2, p. 90.

HADDEN (J. C.). *Haydn.* London: J. M. Dent & Co. 1934. By permission also of Messrs. E. P. Dutton & Co., Inc.

+(130) p. 148.

HAGGARD (*Sir* H. Rider). *The Days of my Life.* 2 vols. Edited by C. J. Longman. London: Longmans, Green & Co. 1926. By permission also of Lady Haggard and Messrs. A. P. Watt & Son, London.

 (132) Vol. 2, pp. 92–93.
 (133)   „   p. 166.

HALDANE (E. S.). *Descartes: His Life and Times.* London: John Murray. 1905.
(134) p. 361.
HAMILTON (*Sir* William). *Lectures on Metaphysics and Logic.* 4 vols. Edinburgh and London: William Blackwood & Sons. 1859–60.
+(135) Vol. 1, p. 255.
+(136) „ p. 257.
HAMMERTON (*Sir* John Alexander). *Barrie: The story of a genius.* London: Sampson Law, Marston & Co. 1929.
+(137) p. 150.
HAMERTON (P. G.). *The Life of J. M. W. Turner, R.A.* London: Seeley, Jackson & Halliday. 1879.
(138) pp. 75, 82, 87.
(139) p. 134.
(140) p. 180.
(141) p. 190.
HARDING (Rosamond E. M.). *Towards a Law of Creative Thought.* 'Psyche Monographs,' No. 7. London: Kegan Paul, Trench, Trubner & Co. 1936.
(142) pp. 131–38.
HELLBORN (K. von). *Life of Franz Schubert.* 2 vols. Translated by A. D. Coleridge. London: Longmans, Green & Co. 1869.
(143) Vol. 2, pp. 75–76.
+(144) „ p. 158.
+(145) „ pp. 160–61.
HERON-ALLEN (E.). *Giuseppe Tartini.* Article in *Grove's Dictionary of Music.* 3rd edition. Edited by H. C. Colles. Vol. 5. London: Macmillan & Co., Ltd. 1928.
(146) p. 268.
(147) p. 270.
HOGARTH (Basil). *The Technique of Novel Writing.* London: John Lane, The Bodley Head, Ltd., 1934.
+(147A) p. 51.
+(147B) p. 141.
HOLLAND (Clive, M.B.E.). *Thomas Hardy, O.M., The Man, his Works and the Land of Wessex.* London: Herbert Jenkins. 1933.
+(148) p. 79.
(149) p. 119.
HOUSMAN (A. E.). *The Name and Nature of Poetry.* London and Cambridge: Cambridge University Press. 1933.
+(150) pp. 49–50.
HUCHON (Rene). *George Crabbe and his Times.* English Translation by F. Clarke. London: John Murray. 1907.
(151) p. 400.
HUGO (Victor). *Intellectual Autobiography* (Postscriptum de ma vie). Translated by L. O'Rourke. Funk & Wagnalls Co., London (27a, Farringdon Street) and New York (354–60, Fourth Avenue). 1907.
+(152) pp. 124–25.
HULL (A. Eaglefield). *Scriabin.* London: Kegan Paul, Trench, Trubner & Co. 1916.
(153) p. 251.
HUNT (Leigh). *Lord Byron and some of his Contemporaries.* London. 1828.
(154) pp. 37–38.
INGRAM (J. H.). *Edgar Allan Poe.* 2 vols. London: John Hogg. 1880.
(155) Vol. 1, pp. 155–56.

JAHN (Otto). *Life of Mozart.* 3 vols. Translated by P. D. Townsend. London: Novello, Ewer & Co. 1882.

 (156) Vol. 2, pp. 419–20.
 (157) " pp. 423–24.
 (158) " p. 440.
 (159) " p. 441.

JAMES (Henry). *The American.* 'New York Edition' of the *Novels and Tales.* Vol. 2. London: Macmillan & Co. 1909.

 +(160) Preface, p. xi.

JEAN-AUBRY (G.). *Joseph Conrad: Life and Letters.* 2 vols. London: William Heinemann, Ltd. 1927.

 +(161). Vol. 1, p. 301.

J. (E.). *Life and Letters of Sidney Dobell.* Edited by E. J. 2 vols. London: Smith Elder & Co. 1878. By permission of Messrs. John Murray, London.

 +(162) Vol. 1, p. 105 (extract from a letter to *Rev.* G. Gilfillan, May, 1849).

 +(163) " pp. 196–97.
 +(164) " p. 447.

JONSON (Ben). *Discoveries made upon Men and Matter.* Vol. 9 of *The Works of Ben Jonson with Notes, etc. and a Biographical Memoir* by W. Gifford. 9 vols. London. 1816.

 +(165) pp. 237–278.

KALISCHER (Dr. A. C.). *Beethoven's Letters.* Edited by Dr. Kalischer and translated by J. S. Shedlock. London: J. M. Dent & Sons, Ltd. 1909. See BEETHOVEN.

KEATS (John). *The Letters of John Keats.* Edited by M. Buxton Forman. 2nd edition. London: Oxford University Press. 1935.

 +(166) p. 72, letter 32.
 +(167) pp. 227–28, letter 93.

KEBBEL (T. E.). *Life of George Crabbe,* 'Great Writers Series.' London: Walter Scott. 1888.

 (168) p. 88.
 +(169) p. 100.

KENNEDY (W. S.). *John G. Whittier.* New York: Funk & Wagnalls Co. 1892.

 (170) pp. 225–226.
 (171) p. 295.

—— *Reminiscences of Walt Whitman.* London: Alexander Gardiner. 1896.

 +(172) p. 24.

KIPLING (Rudyard). *Something of Myself.* London: Macmillan & Co. 1937.

 +(173). pp. 208–09.

KNIGHT (W.). *Prose Works of William Wordsworth.* Edited by W. Knight. 2 vols. London: Macmillan & Co., Ltd. 1896. See WORDSWORTH.

LAMB (Charles). *Last Essays of Elia.* Vol. 4 of 'The Life, Letters and Writings of Charles Lamb' edited by P. Fitzgerald. Enfield edition. London: T. & A. Constable [1924].

 +(174) pp. 164–65, 'Popular Fallacies XV.'

LAWTON (F.). *Balzac.* London: Grant Richards. 1910. The Richards Press, Ltd.

 +(175) p. 92.
 (176) p. 124.
 +(177) p. 373.

LEE (*Mrs.* R., formerly *Mrs.* T. Ed. Bowdich). *Memoirs of Baron Cuvier.* London. 1833.

 (178) p. 289.

LESLIE (C. R.). *Memoirs of the Life of John Constable, Esq., R.A.* 2nd edition. London: Longman, Brown, Green & Longmans, 1845. Messrs. Longmans, Green & Co., Ltd.
+(179) p. 93.
+(180) p. 307.
LOCKHART (J. G.). *Memoirs of Sir Walter Scott.* 5 vols. London: Macmillan & Co., Ltd. 1900.
(181) Vol. 3, p. 280.
LOCKSPEISER (E.). *Debussy.* London: J. M. Dent & Sons. 1936. By permission of Messrs. E. P. Dutton & Co., Inc.
(182) p. 20.
+(183) p. 106 (concerning 'La Chute de la maison Usher').
+(184) p. 108.
+(185) p. 274.
+(186) p. 276.
LOWELL (A.). *John Keats.* 2 vols. London: Jonathan Cape, Ltd. [1924].
+(187) Vol. 1, pp. 501–502.
LUCAS-DUBRETON (J.). *Alexandre Dumas.* Translated by M. C. Darnton. London: Thornton Butterworth, Ltd. 1929.
(188) p. 135.
(189) p. 144.
LUDOVICI (A. M.). *Personal Reminiscences of Auguste Rodin.* London: John Murray. 1926.
+(190) p. 70.
MAINE (Basil). *Elgar, His Life and Works.* London: G. Bell & Sons. 1933.
+(191) Vol. 1, p. 117.
+(192) „ p. 268.
MAUCLAIR (C.). *Auguste Rodin.* Translated by C. Black. London: Duckworth & Co. 1905.
(193) pp. 14–15.
MAUDE (Aylmer). *The Life of Tolstoy: Later years.* London: Constable & Co., Ltd. 1910.
+(194) p. 343.
MARCHANT (James). *Alfred Russel Wallace.* 2 vols. London: Cassell & Co. 1916.
+(195) Vol. 1, p. 116.
+(196) „ p. 117.
+(197) Vol. 2, p. 242.
MARROT (M. V.). *Life and Letters of John Galsworthy.* London: William Heinemann, Ltd. 1935.
(198) p. 588.
+(199) p. 733.
MCKENZIE (A. L.). *The George Sand-Gustave Flaubert Letters.* Translated by A. L. McKenzie. London: Duckworth & Co., Ltd. 1922.
+(200) pp. 32–33, letter XXXIII.
+(201) p. 41, letter XL.
+(202) p. 116, letter CI.
+(203) p. 323, letter CCLXXX.
+(204) pp. 359–60, letter CCCV.
MEDWIN (Thomas). *Life of Percy Bysshe Shelley*, with Introduction and Commentary by H. Buxton Forman. London: Oxford University Press. 1913.
+(205) pp. 27–28.
+(206) p. 75.
(207) p. 89.
MÉGROZ (R. L.). *Dante Gabriel Rossetti.* London: Faber & Gwyer [1928]. Messrs. Faber & Faber, Ltd.
+(208) pp. 101–102.

136   AN ANATOMY OF INSPIRATION

MELVILLE (Lewis). *William Makepeace Thackeray*. London: Ernest
        Benn, Ltd. 1927.
  +(209) pp. 253–54.
  +(210) p. 408.
MERSMANN (H.). *Letters of Wolfgang Amadeus Mozart*, selected and edited
        by Hans Mersmann. Translated by M. M. Bozman. Lon-
        don: J. M. Dent & Sons. 1928. By permission also of
        Messrs. E. P. Dutton & Co., Inc.
  +(211). Preface, pp. vii–viii.
MEYNELL (E.). *Corot and his Friends*. London: Methuen & Co., Ltd.
        1908.
  +(212) p. 97.
  +(213) pp. 100–01.
MILLAIS (J. G.). *Life and Letters of Sir John Everett Millais*. 2 vols.
        London: Methuen & Co., Ltd. 1899.
    (214) Vol. 1, pp. 32–33.
  +(215)   „   p. 158.
    (216) Vol. 2, p. 339.
MONTMASSON (Joseph-Marie). *Invention and the Unconscious*. Translated
        by H. Stafford Hatfield. London: 'International Library of
        Psychology.' Kegan Paul, Trench, Trubner & Co. 1931.
    (217) p. 1.
MOORE (Thomas). *Memoirs, Journal and Correspondence*. Edited and
        abridged from the first edition by Lord John Russell, M.P.
        London: Longman, Green, Longman & Roberts, 1860.
        (Messrs. Longmans, Green & Co., Ltd.)
  +(218) p. 193.
—— *Poetical Works*. Oxford edition. Edited by A. D. Godley.
        London: Oxford University Press. 1910.
  +(219) pp. 506–07—*Rhymes on the Road*. (Introductory Rhymes).
—— *Works of Lord Byron with his Letters and Journals and his Life*.
        14 vols. London: John Murray. 1832, 1833.
  +(220) Vol. 2, p. 247, letter 141.
  +(221) Vol. 5, p. 281,   „   466.
  +(222)   „   p. 285,   „   468.
MORGAN (Louise) *Writers at Work*. The Dolfin Books. London:
        Chatto and Windus, 1931.
  +(222A) p. 6.
  +(222B) p. 38.
  +(222C) pp. 45–46.
  +(222D) p. 49.
MUIRHEAD (J. P.). *Life of James Watt*. 2nd edition. London: John
        Murray. 1859.
    (223) p. 513.
MURRAY (R. H.). *Science and Scientists of the Nineteenth Century*. London:
        Sheldon Press. 1925.
  +(224) p. 233.
MUSSET (Paul de). *The Biography of Alfred de Musset*. Translated by
        H. W. Preston. Boston: Roberts Brothers. 1877.
    (225) pp. 121–22, see also p. 130.
  +(226) p. 162.
NEVINSON (H. W.). *Life of Friedrich Schiller*. 'Great Writers' Series.'
        London: Walter Scott. 1889.
    (227) pp. 188–89.
NEWMAN (Ernest). *The Life of Richard Wagner*. 2 vols. London:
        Cassell & Co. 1933, 1937.
    (228) Vol. 1, p. 469.
    (229) Vol. 2, pp. 360–61.
    (230)   „   p. 368.
    (231)   „   p. 397.

NEWMARCH (Rosa). *Tchaikovsky.* Edited by E. Evans, *senr.* London: William Reeves. 1908.
  (232) p. 15.
  (233) p. 95.
NIECKS (F.). *Frederick Chopin.* 2 vols. London: Novello, Ewer & Co. 1888. Messrs. Novello & Co., Ltd.
+(234) Vol. 2, p. 132.
+(235)   "   p. 337 (Extract from *Madame* Streicher's recollections of Chopin).
ORR (*Mrs.* Sutherland). *Life and Letters of Robert Browning.* New edition, revised and in part re-written by F. G. Kenyon. London: Smith, Elder & Co. 1908. By permission of Messrs. John Murray, London.
+(236) p. 232.
  (237) pp. 250–251.
  (238) See p. 361.
PEARSON (Karl). *Life, Letters and Labours of Francis Galton.* 4 vols. London and Cambridge: Cambridge University Press. 1914, 1924, 1930.
  (239) Vol. 3A, p. 115.
PEBODY (C.). *Authors at Work.* London: William Allen & Co. 1872.
+(240) pp. 92–94.
  (241) p. 100.
+(242) p. 175.
PENNELL (E. R.) and (J.). *Life of James McNeill Whistler.* London: William Heinemann, 1191.
  (243) p. 113.
PERIER (*Madame*). *The Life of Mr. Paschal* [written by his Sister, *Madame* Perier] with his letters relating to the Jesuits. 2 vols. Translated by W. A., London. 1744.
  (244) Vol. 1, pp. xxx–xxxi.
PERRY (R. Barton). *The Thought and Character of William James.* 2 vols. London: Oxford University Press [1935]. By permission of Messrs. Little, Brown & Co., Boston, U.S.A. and the Oxford University Press, London.
+(245) Vol. 2, p. 676.
PHILLIPS (John). *The Life of Mr. John Milton* in *The Early Lives of Milton.* Edited with introduction and notes by Helen Darbishire. London: Constable & Co. 1932.
+(246) p. 33.
PLATO. *Apology.* Translated by F. J. Church, contained in *The Trial and Death of Socrates.* 'Golden Treasury Series.' London: Macmillan & Co., Ltd. 1927.
+(247) p. 44.
POE (Edgar Allan). *Works.* 4 vols. Edited by J. H. Ingram. Edinburgh and London: Adam and Charles Black, Ltd. 1875.
+(248) Vol. 3, pp. 266–67 (Philosophy of Composition).
+(249)   "   pp. 268–78 (*ibid.*).
POINCARÉ (Henri). *Science and Method.* English translation by F. Maitland. London: Thomas Nelson & Sons [1914].
+(250) p. 56 (Chapter on 'Mathematical Discovery').
+(215) p. 63. do.
PRIESTLEY (*Dr.* Joseph). *Memoirs of Dr. Joseph Priestley* to 1795 with a continuation by his son, J. Priestley. Reprinted from the edition of 1809. London: H. R. Alleson. 1904.
+(252) p. 69, § 174.
+(253) p. 100.
  (254) p. 118.

RAYLEIGH (Robert John Strutt *Lord*). *John William Strutt, Third Baron Rayleigh, O.M., F.R.S.* London: Edward Arnold & Co. 1924.
    (255) p. 164.
    (256) p. 257.

READE (C. L.) and (*Rev.* C.). *Charles Reade: A Memoir.* 2 vols. London: Chapman & Hall. 1887.
    (257) Vol. 1, p. 328.
    (258) Vol. 2, p. 187.

REDDING (Cyrus). *Fifty Years' Recollections Literary and Personal.* 3 vols. 2nd and revised edition. London: Charles J. Skeet. 1858.
  +(259) Vol. 1, p. 199.

REED (W. H.). *Elgar as I knew Him.* London: Victor Gollancz, Ltd. 1936.
  +(260) pp. 128–30.

REISER (A.). *Albert Einstein.* London: Thornton Butterworth, Ltd. 1931.
  +(261) pp. 116–17.

REYNOLDS (*Sir* Joshua). *Literary Works.* 3 vols. London: T. Cadell, *jun.* and W. Davies. 1798.
  +(262) Vol. 1, p. 147, 6th Discourse.
  +(263) Vol. 2, p. 103, 12th Discourse.
  +(264)   "   pp. 114–17, 13th Discourse.

—— *Literary Works*, with a Memoir by H. W. Beechey. 2 vols. London. 1835.
  +(265) Vol. 1, pp. 116–17 (extract from a quotation from W. Northcote, R.A.).

RHYDDERCH (D.). *Jane Austen.* London: Jonathan Cape. 1932.
    (266) p. 139.

RIBOT (T.). *Essay on the Creative Imagination.* Translated by A. H. N. Baron. London: Kegan Paul, Trench, Trubner & Co. 1906.
  +(267) p. 264.

RICHARDSON (J.). *Explanatory Notes and Remarks on Milton's Paradise Lost with the Life of the Author*, contained in *The Early Lives of John Milton*, edited by H. Darbishire. London: Constable & Co., Ltd. 1932.
  +(268) p. 291.

RIMSKY-KORSAKOFF (N. A.). *My Musical Life.* Translated by J. A. Joffe and edited by Carl van Vechten. London: Martin Secker. 1924. By permission of Messrs. Martin Secker & Warburg, Ltd., London; and Messrs. Alfred A. Knopf, New York.
  +(269) p. 193.
  +(270) p. 292.

RIVERS (W. H. R.). *Conflict and Dream.* 'International Library of Psychology.' Kegan Paul, Trench, Trubner & Co. 1923.
  +(271) p. 7.

ROSSETTI (William Michael). *Preraphaelite Diaries and Letters.* Edited by W. M. Rossetti. London: Hurst & Blackett. 1900.
  +(272) pp. 262–63 (From III Journal kept by Rossetti, 1849–53).
—— *Rossetti Papers*, 1862 to 1870. London: Sands & Co., Ltd. 1903.
  +(273) p. 302.

RUSKIN (John) *Dilecta*, Vol. xxxv of 'Complete Works' edited by *Sir* E. T. Cook and A. Wedderburn. London: George Allen & Unwin, Ltd. 1908.
    (274) pp. 598–601.

RUSSELL (G. B.). *The Letters of William Blake*, together with a *Life* by Tatham. Edited by G. B. Russell. London: Methuen & Co., Ltd. 1906. See BLAKE.

SAND (George) *Letters*. 3 vols. Translated and edited by R. Ledos de Beaufort. London: Ward & Downey. 1886.
+ (275) Vol. 1, p. 261.
+ (276) Vol. 3, p. 315.

SANDARS (M. F.). *George Sand*. London: Robert Holden & Co. 1927.
(277) p. 17.

SASSOON (Siegfried) *On Poetry*. Arthur Skemp Memorial Lecture. Bristol: University Press, 1939.
+ (277A) p. 6.
+ (277B) p. 19.

SCHMITZ (L. D.). *Correspondence between Schiller and Goethe*. 2 vols. Translated from the 3rd German edition by L. D. Schmitz. London: George Bell & Sons. 1877, 1879.
+ (278) Vol. 1, p. 154, letter 161.
+ (279)   „   p. 353,   „   342.

SCOTT (*Sir* Walter). *Journal, 1825–32*. Edinburgh: Douglas & Foulis. 1927.
+ (280) p. 66.
+ (281) p. 113, see also p. 200.
+ (282) p. 397.

SENCOURT (R. E.). *Life of George Meredith*. London: Chapman & Hall, Ltd. 1929.
(283) p. 183.
+ (284) p. 214.

SHARP (W.). *Life of Robert Browning*. 'Great Writers.' London: Walter Scott. 1890.
(285) pp. 61–62.

SHAWCROSS (J.). *Coleridge's Biographia Literaria*. Oxford: Clarendon Press. 1907. See COLERIDGE.

SHELLEY (Percy Bysshe). *Prose Works*. 4 vols. Edited by H. Buxton Forman. London: Reeves & Turner. 1880.
+ (286) Vol. 3, p. 137 (From 'A Defence of Poetry').

SIDNEY (*Sir* Philip). *An Apologie for Poetrie*. English reprints edited by Edward Arber. London: Alex Murray & Son. 1868.
+ (287) pp. 24–25.

SKENE (J.). *Memories of Sir Walter Scott*. Edited by Basil Thomson. London: John Murray. 1909.
(288) pp. 91–92.

SMILES (Samuel). *Lives of the Engineers*. 3 vols. London: John Murray. 1861.
(289) Vol. 1, p. 473.

SMITH (G. Barnett). *Victor Hugo*. London: Ward & Downey. 1885.
(290) p. 269.

SOUTHEY (*Rev.* C. C.). *Life and Correspondence of Southey*. 6 vols. London: Longman, Brown Green & Longmans, 1849–50. (Messrs. Longmans, Green & Co., Ltd.)
+ (291) Vol. 2, p. 264.
(292) Vol. 6, p. 17.

SPEARMAN (C.). *Creative Mind*. 'Contemporary Library of Psychology.' London: Nisbet & Co. 1930.
(293) p. 77.

SPENCER (Herbert). *Autobiography*. 2 vols. London: Williams & Norgate. 1904. By permission of the Rationalist Press Association, Ltd., London.
+ (294) Vol. 2, pp. 435–36.

SPITTA (Philipp). *The Life of Bach.* 3 vols. English translation by Clara
        Bell and J. A. Fuller-Maitland. London: Novello, Ewer &
        Co. 1884, 1885.
  (295) Vol. 3, pp. 262–63.

STANDISH (F. H.). *Life of Voltaire.* London. 1821.
  (296) p. 389.

STEVENS (A.). *Madame de Staël.* 2 vols. London: John Murray. 1881.
  (297) Vol. 2, pp. 230–31.
  (298)   „   p. 240.

STEVENSON (R. L.). *Works.* 25 vols. Swanston edition. London:
        Chatto & Windus. 1912.
  (299) Vol. 16, pp. 187–89 (A Chapter on Dreams).
  (300)   „   pp. 335–37.

STEWART (Dugald). *Biographical Memoirs of Adam Smith, LL.D., of
        Thomas Robertson, D.D., and of Thomas Reid, D.D. Read
        before the Royal Soc. of Edinburgh,* Edinburgh [1810?].
  +(301) p. 107, *Note.*
  +(302) pp. 113–14.

ST. JOHN (B.). *Montaigne the Essayist.* 2 vols. London: Chapman &
        Hall, Ltd. 1858.
  +(303) Vol. 2, p. 103.

STUCKENBERG (J. H. W.). *Life of Immanuel Kant.* London: Macmillan &
        Co., Ltd. 1882.
  (304) pp. 80–81.
  (305) p. 109.
  (306) pp. 146–47.
  (307) p. 149.

STUKELEY (*Dr.* William). *Memoirs of Sir Isaac Newton's Life.* Edited
        by A. Hastings White. London: Taylor & Francis. 1936.
  (308) Introduction, p. xiv.
  +(309) pp. 19–20.

SWEDENBORG (Emanuel). *Heaven and Hell.* Published for the Sweden-
        borg Society by Penguin Books, Ltd. 1938. By permission
        of The Swedenborg Society. London.
  +(310) p. 117, § 262 (from 'Writing in Heaven').

TALLENTYRE (S. G.). *Voltaire in his Letters.* London: John Murray. 1919.
  +(311) p. 66.

TARVER (J. C.). *Gustave Flaubert as seen in his Works and Correspondence.*
        Westminster: Archibald Constable & Co. 1895. (Messrs.
        Constable & Co., Ltd.)
  +(312) p. 67.
  +(313) p. 196.
  +(314) p. 287.

TCHAIKOVSKY (Modeste). *The Life and Letters of Peter Ilich Tchaikovsky.*
        Edited from the Russian by Rosa Newmarch. London:
        John Lane, The Bodley Head, Ltd. 1906.
  +(315) p. 108.
  +(316) pp. 274–75.
  +(317) p. 281.
  +(318) pp. 306–309.
  +(319) pp. 311–12.
  +(320) pp. 405 and 441.
  +(321) pp. 607–08.

TENNYSON (Hallam, *Lord*) *Alfred, Lord Tennyson: A Memoir.* 2 vols.
        London: Macmillan & Co. 1897.
  (322) Vol. 2, p. 210 (Period, 1874–75).
  +(323)   „   p. 496 (Personal recollections of F. T. Palgrave).

THACKERAY (W. M.). *The Works of W. M. Thackeray*, with biographical introductions by his daughter, Anne Ritchie. 13 vols. London: Smith, Elder & Co. 1898–99. By permission of Messrs. John Murray. London.

+(324) Vol. VIII. *The Newcomes*, Introduction, p. xxii.
+(325)   „   „   „   pp. xxxvi–xxxvii.
+(326) Vol. IX. *Christmas Books*, Introduction, p. xlvii.
 (327) Vol. X. *The Virginians*, Introduction, p. xxxvii.
 (328) Vol. XII. *Lovel, the Widower*, Introduction, p. xiv.
+(329)   „   „   „   p. xxv.
 (330)   „   „   „   p. xxvii.
+(331)   „   *Roundabout Papers*, pp. 374–75.

THAYER (A. W.). *Life of Ludwig van Beethoven*. 3 vols. Edited and revised by H. E. Krehbiel. New York: Beethoven Association. 1921.

 (332) p. 316.

THOMPSON (S. P.). *The Life of Lord Kelvin of Largs*. 2 vols. London: Macmillan & Co., Ltd. 1910.

+(333) Vol. 2, p. 1096.
+(334)   „ p. 1126.

THOMSON (*Sir* Joseph John). *Recollections and Reflections*. London: G. Bell & Sons. 1936.

+(335) p. 82.

THORNBURY (Walter). *Life of J. M. W. Turner, R.A.* 2 vols. London: Hurst & Blackett. 1862.

+(336) Vol. 1, pp. 235–36.

THORPE (T. E.). *Joseph Priestley*. London: J. M. Dent & Co. 1906.

 (337) p. 74.

TOLAND (John). *The Life of John Milton* contained in *The Early Lives of Milton*. Edited by H. Darbishire. London: John Constable & Co., Ltd. 1932.

+(338) p. 194.

TOYNBEE (P.) and WHIBLEY (L.). *Correspondence of Thomas Gray*. Edited by Toynbee & Whibley. Oxford: Clarendon Press. 1935. See GRAY.

TRELAWNY (E. J.). *Records of Shelley, Byron and the Author*. 2 vols. London: B. M. Pickering. 1878.

+(339) Vol. 1, pp. 104 and 170.
+(340)   „ pp. 107–08.
+(341) Vol. 2, p. 84.

TREVELYAN (*Sir* George Otto). *Life and Letters of Lord Macaulay*. New Edition. 2 vols. London: Longmans, Green & Co. 1878.

+(342) Vol. 2, p. 128.

TURNBULL (A.). *Coleridge's Biographia Epistolaris*. Edited by A. Turnbull. London: G. Bell & Sons, Ltd. 1907. See COLERIDGE.

TURNER (W. J.). *Berlioz: The Man and his Work*. London: J. M. Dent & Sons. 1934.

 (343) p. 242–43.

VALLERY-RADOT (R.). *The Life of Pasteur*. Translated by R. L. Devonshire. 2 vols. Westminster: Archibald Constable & Co. 1902. Messrs. Constable & Co., Ltd.

+(344) Vol. 1, p. 199.
 (345) Vol. 2, p. 33.

VIZETELLY (E. A.). *Émile Zola*. London: John Lane, The Bodley Head. 1904.

 (346) pp. 369–371.
 (347) See also pp. 372–73.

WAGENKNECHT (E.). *Mark Twain: The Man and his Work.* New Haven: Yale University Press, and London: Oxford University Press. 1935.

+(348) p. 78.

WAGNER (Richard). *Letters.* Selected and edited by Wilhelm Altmann. Translated by M. M. Bozman. 2 vols. London: J. M. Dent & Sons, Ltd. 1927. By permission also of Messrs. E. P. Dutton & Co., Inc.

+(349) Vol. 1, p. 197 (letter to Franz Liszt).
+(350)   ″   p. 342.
+(351) Vol. 2, p. 116.

WATTS (M. S.). *George Frederick Watts.* 3 vols. London: Macmillan & Co., Ltd. 1912.

+(352) Vol. 1, pp. 234–35.
+(353)   ″   p. 65.
+(354) Vol. 2, p. 114.

WEBER (*Baron* Max Maria von). *Carl Maria von Weber.* Translated by J. Palgrave Simpson. 2 vols. London: Chapman & Hall, Ltd. 1865.

+(355) Vol. 2, pp. 81–84.
+(356)   ″   pp. 292–94.

WILSON (G.). *The Life of the Hon. Henry Cavendish.* London: Cavendish Society. 1851.

+(357) p. 20.
+(358) p. 165.

WORDSWORTH (C.). *Memoirs of William Wordsworth.* 2 vols. London: Edward Moxon. 1851.

+(359) Vol. 2, p. 476–77.

WORDSWORTH (Dorothy) *Journals of Dorothy Wordsworth.* Edited by William Knight. London: Macmillan & Co., Ltd., 1924.

+(359A) p. 86.
+(359B) p. 124.

WORDSWORTH (William). *Prose Works.* Edited by W. Knight. 2 vols. London: Macmillan & Co., Ltd. 1896.

+(360) Vol. 1, p. 68 (Preface to the Lyrical Ballads).

WRIGHT (T.). *Life of Walter Pater.* 2 vols. London: Everett & Co. 1907.
 (361) Vol. 2, pp. 135–36.

YEATS (W. B.). *Essays.* Collected Edition. London: Macmillan & Co., Ltd. 1924.

+(362) pp. 196–97 ('Symbolism of Poetry').
+(363) pp. 248–49 ('The Return of Ulysses').
+363A) p. 239 ('The Moods').

ZIMMERN (H.). *Arthur Schopenhauer.* London: Longmans, Green & Co. 1876.

 (364) p. 49.
+(365) p. 170

Index